THE
DIVIDING LINE

INDIALOG PUBLICATIONS PVT. LTD.

THE
DIVIDING LINE

Jean Arasanayagam

INDIALOG PUBLICATIONS PVT. LTD.

Published by

Indialog Publications Pvt. Ltd.
O - 22, Lajpat Nagar II
New Delhi - 110024
Tel.: 91-11-6839936/6320504
Fax: 91-11-6935221
Internet Addresses: http://www.indialogpublications.com
                    http://www.onepageclassic.com

First Published June, 2002
Copyright © Jean Arasanayagam, 2002

Cover Painting *Mother & Child* by Richard Gabriel. Courtesy
The Heritage Collection, R. Rajamahendran.

Printed at Chaman Offset Prints, Darya Ganj, New Delhi.

ISBN 81-87981-22-9

Makarand Paranjape, Meenakshi Mukherjee,
Nihal Fernando, R. Rajamahendran,
Radhika Coomaraswamy and my daughters
Devi and Parvathi.

ACKNOWLEDGMENTS

The story "The Wisdom Mantra" first appeared in *Satyn*. "The Adoption" first appeared in *Options*. "The Cry of the Kite" appeared in *The Cry of the Kite*, a collection of short stories by Jean Arasanayagam; *An Anthology of Contemporary Sri Lankan Short Stories*, edited by Ashley Halpe; and in *Peacocks and Dreams* published by Navrang. My thanks to R. Rajamahendran for granting permission to use the painting from his Heritage Collection and to the artist for his inspiring painting.

CONTENTS

THE GARDEN PARTY

Kundasale 1988

Half a century has passed since the event recorded in my diaries took place. My sister Cathy and I are now all alone. This convent run by Roman Catholic nuns is our place of refuge.

I have preserved many things from the past. My memories of those momentous years of my life in pre-war England and Europe, in the year 1938 on the eve of the outbreak of the Second World War are carefully handwritten, day by day, month by month on the pages of exercise books. They are preserved to this day so that I can always recall the experiences which are still fresh in my mind.

For me, it had been a saga of self-discovery. I was free, independent, not yet married and for that age and time an emancipated woman.

In England, in Europe, no one cared about who I was. I did not have to be self-conscious about my birth. I was smart, intelligent, educated and I possessed a piquant air of charm and beauty, I had many admirers, made many friends wherever I went. There were no trammels to bind me. I basked in the admiration of those whom I met on the outward voyage from Ceylon which was then under colonial rule.

At the back of my mind I always felt a sense of guilt. I suffered in those early years far more than Cathy did. We were taken away from our mother after our father, the English planter went away. Even when we grew up, when we reached the age of understanding, we had to follow a way of life where we would fit into colonial society. The moral principles of Christianity were inculcated in us by the missionaries and guided our vocations as teachers.

We concealed our mother's existence in our lives. Shut her out. Together with her people. We hid our birthright.

It is now too late, too late to make amends. When I look back on the past I perceive that it was that historical epoch that molded our very lives. We were ashamed of that divided inheritance.

What does it all matter now? We are just minute flecks of foam tossed on those deep waves on an unknown ocean. For some, those oceans and those voyages were chartered. They had a purpose, those historical voyages that were embarked on and somewhere along the line in the process of acquiring territory, engaging in trade and commerce, our birth and that of thousands of others, took place. We were left alone when the trophies of the Empire were no longer important. As we are now. Alone. All alone.

There is no necessity to vindicate that birthright. The voyage took me away from the island but brought me home again where I truly belong. It was a long, long search but I found myself, after the years had passed, shedding the bitterness and rancor I felt in being abandoned by the father who named us, making us forget our mother. We could never return to either of them. Nor could they claim us again.

London 1938

I have now reached where I want to be. Accepted as somebody. With a social identity. It was an uphill task. I began from nowhere. A divided ancestry. Part British. The other, sprung from this native soil. My father, the imperial representative of the British Raj, a planter. My mother, a Sinhala woman from the village lying on the outskirts of the upcountry tea estate. At the height of the Empire. Its heyday.

My sister and I. Of the two of us, I was the more dominant. I had to make a decision. To move away from one part of my inheritance, to belong to this new social order. The upward trend. Or to be dragged into darkness and obscurity, wedged into that historical niche of the Empire.

I was from a very early stage aware that there was a difference. Everyone looked up to my father, the white man. Power and authority were embodied in him. I wanted to belong to that part of my identity, one that would ensure me recognition and a respected place in society. Once I embarked on this path there would be no turning back. It meant that I had to reject one part of my identity – my mother's way of life. The Empire compelled me along the route and this route brought me here, to London in the year 1938 when I became a mature student at the Institute of Education in the University of London. I would explore every corner of the inheritance that was foisted on me. I would rediscover the Empire and what it stood for in my life dictating where I would take up my stance.

When the invitation to the Garden Party at Buckingham Palace arrived I was pleased that I was one of those singled out to be present. Many of the guests would belong to the British Colonies. The Commonwealth would be represented in all its variegated hues. I made up my mind to attire myself in clothes that I thought suitable to the role I would play in the future. I was aware however that allegiance to one strand of my inheritance would lead to betrayal of the other. I had no alternative. I followed my father's path. I carried his name. I was baptized in his faith. "Marian Laing." A name that revealed the colonial part of me.

I was excited at the thought of attending the Garden Party. My sister-in-law to be Sophie, belonged to a different strand of colonization. The respected Dutch Burgher community. She was also in London studying with me. The invitations were for us both.

In my diary every detail of that colonial exploration has been meticulously recorded, I observe that I had summed up that occasion in one phrase. "A very successful evening."

Successful? It was my acceptance into that enclave, my recognition, the fact that I had been able to mingle freely with the now growing assertiveness of my identity that had made me feel at ease in the company gathered there. I moved among the English aristocracy and the other visitors from the colonies, including my own compatriots from Ceylon. For me, it was an imperial tableau. I had been able to glimpse the icons of the Empire. We were both spectators and participants. No one questioned my birth, that I was of Eurasian blood. I was from the colony of Ceylon where so many colonial expeditions had taken place. The color of my skin was naturally a part of that colonial experience of the Empire Builders.

I had first of all to decide what I was to wear to the Garden Party. On board the *Van St. Aldegoude*, the ship I had made the voyage on to reach England I had worn a sari at a Fancy Dress Party. It made me different, where everybody looked upon me as a woman from the mysterious East. I knew that people had all kinds of fantasies about women like myself. We embodied what was different. We were exotic, orientals.

The silk sari, clinging to my body singled me out from the others wearing an assortment of costumes or disguises. I wanted people to conjecture about me. I carried an aura of glamor. The rest of the time on board I wore tailored suits and blouses which suited my western hairstyle and makeup. But here, at the Garden Party I did not want to be different. I did not want to cultivate an air of mystique. I did not want to direct the attention of the invitees to myself but to mingle with the crowds. Not to flaunt myself. For this purpose I was going to get myself a brand new outfit.

Bond Street, that's where I would shop. I sallied forth with my entire month's allowance in my handbag. Marshall and Snelgrove, in my opinion both posh and expensive, was where I bought my dress, hat, handbag, gloves. My footwear, high-heeled (were they Cinderella's slippers) purchased from Lilley and Spinner, fitted my tiny feet to perfection. I rehearsed my role in my room, donning my brand new clothes before arranging them on hangers in my wardrobe, trying them on before the mirror. Fine clothes indeed for the little provincial teacher from that island colony of Ceylon. Now to mingle with those loyal subjects of the Empire. It would surely be a role never envisaged for me by my own father. As children, taking tea with him was a very, very special occasion sitting at high table, our faces reflected on the polished mahogany surface. And then there had been that taking of tea with him at the Grand Hotel in Colombo before his final departure from my life. And now it was tea with Royalty.

For the first time I would be able to view the royal couple and the princesses at close quarters, to be part of that gathering. The garments I eventually chose would give me anonymity. I would protect myself from being vulnerable in this manner. At any rate even at home I had followed the fashions that had come with the colonial masters and I had learned to cut out the patterns and sew them according to the designs in the Ladies Fashion Journals. But here, in London, I could shop in Bond Street, fit myself out in clothes that any Englishwoman would wear on such an occasion.

If only my father could see me! What would he have felt? I had gone beyond, yes, far beyond the limitations and constraints he had imposed upon me at my birth. I would do the things that he had never been able to do himself through my own will to survive. I would teach myself to be wise even if I had to use stratagems to get past those watchful sentries posted at the crossroads of my historical journey.

Yes, I looked forward to the Garden Party at Buckingham Palace. I would enjoy the theatricality of the situation. Myself speaking the lines of my own stage play and enacting my part against the background compounded of all the contrivances of my past. Which side was I to belong to? Perhaps, upto this moment I had followed the will of others, of my father, of the missionaries after my baptism at the font of Methodist Evangelism. Here and now, I could exercise my own choices although I knew that I would never be singled out of that gathering, never be granted the sanction to hold the jeweled crown for one moment in my hands. A crown studded with jewels from those imperial possessions – diamonds, rubies, emeralds, sapphires.

My father had been content being a representative and emissary of the Empire. It was that which gave him a role, stature, identity. My mother did not have to contrive to be anything but herself. Would I have been here today if I had not shared my father's identity? I could not reject it. My own route had been formed by the circumstances of my birth. My education and upbringing had knit me, bonded me to my destinies. Although my mother tongue was a part of my psyche, the more dominant language derived from a dual patriarchy, that of my father's on the one hand and of the Empire on the other. I accepted what was expedient for me to follow. Rejection would make me a silent woman like my mother.

My mind goes back to Passara among the mountains of Uva. Did my father not pursue, besides that imperial mission, his own individual and personal mission as well? But he was sanctioned, oh yes, by that Power, to the annexation of thousands of acres of jungle land. He could command because he too was one of the masters. But there was something more to this whole business, something that those historical documents did not state openly. Who were those children, those girls, those young women whose fathers were planters? The Badulla Girls' Home was a benevolent organization founded by the Missionary Society and the young Eurasians were nurtured and educated there. We, Cathy, and I were among them. It was in the Home that our mother began gradually to move out of our lives, not because she wanted to, she had clung to us until the last, but because separation from her way of life was thought necessary to nurture and civilize us. We too eventually began to step back from those too frequent encounters. There were others like ourselves whose mothers existed in the concealed and hidden darkness, their children taken away from them. They would have no visible monuments erected to their memory after their roles had been explored, the roles of being mistresses to the planters. Their stay in those big estate bungalows were temporary and brief.

The men would embark on their journeys to other colonies in search of fresh fortunes.

Women like my mother were voiceless women, with just a few exceptions. Women who went back to the anonymous dark after they had bedded down with those men. Perhaps their innocence had blinded them to their subjugation. Their bodies had become once more the colonized territory, the acquired territory. Their yield like the land, fruitful. Their influence, in an as yet unenvisaged future, washed away or eroded like the precious topsoil by the torrential rains. The seed that was first strewn on the cleared virgin jungle was prodigal. What was the difference between that of the tea bush and ourselves? The tea bush was pruned regularly or it would have grown into a tall tree. How then would the nimble fingers of those women be able to pick the two leaves and a bud? And those old gnarled trees whose roots went deep down into the earth had sometimes to be uprooted by elephants, so strong, so tenacious they were. Growth was trammeled. So was ours. Our thoughts, our feelings, our emotions pruned and shaped by those who taught us, those who preached to us, those who became our surrogate parents.

The only powerful statement that those voiceless women, our mothers, were allowed to make by the men who had such absolute possession over their bodies, was the birth of their children. Those men, our fathers, needed women just as fire needs kindling, living lonely and isolated in the wilderness, inhabiting a cleared space which was their domain. The women were concubines rather than consorts. What then was their concept of motherhood? To suckle the children until they grew old enough to be taken away? And then our allegiance to our mother country that lay thousands of miles across the seas? What of that? We were under the sway of that bonding. Our minds, our spirits molded and shaped by a different set of loyalties ingrained in us by our birth. Why did the true mother have to be taken away from us before our identity had been legitimized?

My father had not married our mother and yet he had

wanted our lives to be guided by values and principles which had legitimized his own existence in his world, not ours. All my life I would question the source of my birth. I was a strange, new hybrid flower, my colorings, my markings distinctive, different. It had been my mother who was the natural plant, the ungrafted bud, in a sense undefiled. We were not allowed to cling to that vine. The severance had cost us dear. Perhaps my father had considered her influence even a danger. That she would try to change us, take us away with her, back to the village which would claim us all absolutely, leaving the little empire he had carved out bereft of memorials. We were his possessions still. Over our lives he had established an invisible protectorate.

I sometimes think of my mother's body and of the bodies of all those women, from the village, or from the estates where they weeded the land and plucked tea. Their bodies were like the earth from which those forests which once covered that land, had sprung. The forest was a natural growth, primeval, primordial. The tea bushes were different. The seed planted in nurseries, then planted in serrations on the cleared land, was allowed to grow only to a certain height, trimmed and pruned, fragrant with leaf and blossom. Those women-bodies were fertile, fecund, ready to bear fruit naturally yet conditioned in a certain way to be passive, accepting, yielding.

I remember my mother's body that bore a special fragrance about it. It emanated from her skin, her hair, the clothes she wore. A fragrance of fresh earth after the rains had fallen on it, breaking the spell of those sunny days. My mother's hair, the waves smooth and glistening with the king coconut oil which she would pour onto the palm of her hands and press into its abundance. She would then twist it up into a knot and secure it as it lay on the nape of her neck, with a spear-like silver koora. Whenever I was in her presence, seated on her lap, or laying my head against her bosom or sleeping beside her, that fragrance which permeated her body emanated from her very being; the fragrance of the forest, of leaves, of fresh paddy stalks. Her skin was so cool to the touch for each morning she would bathe in the spring water that was piped to the bungalow filling the big aluminium basins and tubs. She wore a silver chain which held the cloth she wrapped round her waist. She never changed the manner of the dress, never wore those long full-skirted gowns that the Englishwomen wore. Round her neck was a silver chain and a tiny pendant studded with red and green stones. Her earlobes were long, weighted down by the cylindrical discs of her earrings. Her clothes always smelt of the dried savendra roots which she kept among the folds.

A feeling of great sadness sweeps over me as I think of her, my mother, a sadness created by that renunciation and by our separation. My childhood was marred, wounded and scarred by the recollection of that pain. What I would see at the Garden Party in the Palace would be glorified motherhood, embodied in the Queen. The Queen Mother. How would that epithet "Queen" make her different to any other mother?

I was a woman divided. Between two cultures. But then, did it not give a third dimension to my nature? I had left my mother behind in the village. Left her with her people, sometimes even forgotten her. Had we, her children not deserted her too? There was no one left to answer her questions – Cathy was teaching too. And here I was long estranged from her way of life, the vice-principal of the very school I myself had studied in. I was far from home now, in England. What were those questions that were left unanswered? "Why had my father left her? Why had we been taken away from her?" She had been a young woman when my father had gone away. Had she lived with another man after that? One of her kind? I sometimes wondered how she withstood that loneliness. Perhaps she had had other children. Even if she had, they were never spoken of nor did I want to know whether I had any other siblings. Were they to fulfil the role that Cathy and I never would? We would never tend her in her old age, the bond was growing weaker and more tenuous with time. We would never go back to the village to claim that inheritance. It would pass into the hands of the true heirs – our bloodline irretrievable.

I was never more aware of my birthright than in this new country. My direct encounter with my father's territory but one which I would have no right to annex. I could have gone in search of his people, of the country village he came from, seek the landmarks which were familiar to him but I would only be searching for a ghost. He was no longer there. My mission was different to his. I sought a different revelation. Had I come to claim an inheritance to which I felt I had a right? Yet how would it change my way of thinking?

My father's mission had been an historical one, sanctioned by the ideas of the Empire. The colonies provided the global markets for that unending flow of trade and commerce. Cathy and I had been nurtured by the prosperity that those revenues had brought in. Even our lives were a part of the territory he had annexed to the Empire. And the Empire itself? It was partly what I had come to explore, although I could form no protectorate over any territory. I was a traveler here. My travels would entail new experiences. I thought of all those colonial travelers, the journeys they made in those far flung parts of the globe, searching, exploring, passing judgment on everything from the landscape to the people and leaving their records in books – diaries, journals, letters ... how would they be deciphered by posterity? As for myself, I too would record what to me is a saga. Those glyphs I make on the page will have meaning only to me – although my personal exploration was annexed to history. Anyone who read my diaries would have to read between the lines and find my hidden self concealed beneath those often banal statements.

How would I view my journey? Unconsciously perhaps it would entail that investigative glimpse into my roots. That line of ancestry which nothing could sever. I had to accept the fact however harsh, that the relationship between my father and mother had been between the subjugator and the subjugated. My childhood had prepared me for the pain that I would suffer, being born out of such a relationship. I would always have to interrogate that inheritance. There was nothing I could do to disguise or conceal that birth.

And now this invitation to take tea with Royalty. The reigning monarchs. The representatives of the mother country. To whom did I own my true allegiance? To my father's people or my mother's? Her people were the subjugated, caught up as they were in that historical process of colonialism. That subjugation was further extended by possession of her body, but when I looked upon my father in my childhood I did not consider him in that light. He was my father. It was he who provided us with security. He was also able to withhold it.

It was then, at that stage, as I was growing up that I began to question both patriarchy and dominance. The two ideas could not be separated. My father's protectorate included the tea estate. He knew all about the value of money. Of banking it. He was one of the founders of the first bank in the Uva province. He provided us with annuities. All from tea. Tea gardens, they were called. The tea bushes growing in ordered rows. The woman plucked the tea – two leaves and a bud. The young women were beautiful, decked in their heavy jewelry, their brilliant cotton cloths wrapped about their bronze, shining limbs, red blue, dark plum purple, peacock green. Their ears were weighted down by the gold discs thrust through the pierced lobes. Wrapped in their thick, black cumblies, hooded like hawks, protected from the mist and cold, they climbed higher and higher on the hillsides to pick the leaf which filled the baskets slung on their backs. Those women had names, women names, names of goddesses too. Their bodies bore strong women odors, their skin and hair moist and dewy as the fresh tea leaf. Woman who were sometimes summoned by the white masters to share their beds, their bodies pressing into the rough cotton of those laundered stone-dashed sheets, rinsed in spring water wrung out and laid to dry on the grass. Beds made of teak, jak, jungle wood. Was there utterance between man and woman? What words passed between them? Or were they both silent caught up in that coital grasp? Master. Mistress. But then, "mistress" was a word that had different connotations. Strange relationships. Often brief. Women who went back to the line rooms, back to pluck tea. Gave birth to children.

Children always named by the father or at baptism, by the missionaries. Names like Grace, Millicent, Mary, Alice, Marian, Helen, Phyllis, Anne. And the sons? George, Arthur, Stephen, Edward, Henry, Robert. Always bore the father's name too – English, Scottish. Names stamped by the insignia of patriarchy.

Ah yes, I knew all about tea. The tea that was allied to that patriarchy. Here, I would sip it from delicate chinaware, special cups I am sure kept apart for those ritual Garden Parties for people like us. That would be used in a succession of tea parties which would reach into posterity decade after decade. Would that fragile and delicate china outlast these monarchs or even the monarchy itself? I felt a pang of nostalgia, thinking of my father's tea estate. I had once thought, as a child, that nothing, that no one, would impinge on that safe world with its boundaries marked out, the jungle kept at bay. I had thought that the house would be an edifice which would last for all time, that those bricks would never crumble nor those rooms echo with the emptiness of my father's departure, the voices of our mother and of ourselves silenced as we too packed our belongings and began on that alternate journey away from my father's self-created empire. I was always searching for something, for someone, perhaps only in memory, from the past. Later on, there was a new Home run by the missionaries. During those days when Fanny Cooke took on the role of surrogate mother.

Our real mothers were there, hidden in the background, sometimes their presence wrested from us for we were powerless to speak and make known our deepest needs. Sometimes the fathers went home on furlough and brought back white women. Wives. Not concubines. Then the Big Bungalow became forbidden ground for the offspring of earlier liaisons. My own father had gone away. We were never to know of any other relationship he had established in yet another part of the Empire.

While here in England, I could if I so desired, question my dual inheritance. I would not renounce my birthright. I was entitled to it. I would explore the foundations of power and ownership which had engendered that identity. In my own way, legitimize it. Restore it's credibility. I would take all I could from this country which owed me those hidden rights. Claim them. My mother had been denied those rights of partnership, equal partnership. Perhaps what I really wanted was not a partnership but an individual identity forged out of those two opposite and opposing roles. Mother. Father. And in-between? Child. I wanted to be a separate entity. I would not allow myself to be pushed into a corner, to be forgotten. Through me, my mother's being, her presence, would live. With the recognition that my father had never completely given her. Did we never question what she had given him? Was it not love that had kept her by his side until he felt he no longer needed her? There was still that unknown territory which he felt the need to explore, land to be surveyed, forest to be cleared and a new dwelling set up.

The Empire had a vast potential, unlimited land without boundaries. In the latter days of his life, alone without our mother and ourselves he would return to his first home. The home which would lead to that grave where his coffin would slide into oblivion. I would not be effaced in that manner. My mother had the right to live in us, her children. As did all those forgotten women whose children were part of them. This fact I would assert without guilt and without shame. There was no need of concealment here. And so, my presence at the Garden Party was to be a vindication of the inheritance thrust upon me.

On the day of the party I groomed myself with care. The significance of the occasion I was still to discover. I gazed at my reflection in the mirror. I was perfectly groomed. To the very fingertips. I, Marian Laing, daughter of Alexander Laing. My own wit and intelligence had provided the sanctions for my exploration at the very heart of the Empire. Never to remain hidden away like my mother. Her sexuality had been used to bring forth the two of us as if we too were extensions of the Empire. I would not allow myself to be relegated to some forgotten niche of history. And when I marry, it will be different. Very different. I shall have it my way. We shall see.

There is so much irony in the way I garb myself. Almost as if I were wrapping myself in the flag of the Empire, to proclaim my allegiance to it. I did not want to appear a replica of my father's people. Speaking in his tongue and addressing him in my imagination, aware at the same time that I possess another bloodline too. And yet a kind of perversity in my imagined thought, burst into spontaneous utterance which had in reality been rehearsed for years.

"Marian Laing, if only your father could see you now!" Poor man – and now I am able to pity him because I have surpassed his abandonment of me. He would be out of place here at this Royal Garden Party. Unable to allow himself to be assimilated in this polyglot crowd. He had always stood out among those over whom he had power on those plantations. He had been away too long from his own kind to find an easy acceptability. Who would want to listen to his travelers' tales? Posterity would look with critical eye upon his enterprises. And in the country village, to which he had ultimately retired to, whom would he speak of his forgotten children? His face, in which I search for resemblances, appears in my mind, his skin weathered by the sun, dry with malarial fevers contacted in the Malayan jungles, his burly frame diminishing with age, no longer able to compel a woman to give her whole life to him. It was left to me to usurp his former power. Vindicating the woman who had been my mother.

I sometimes felt I must search out that country village he had both come from and returned to, find my way to his home, find welcome there. He must have been very much alone as he neared the end. Left with his dreams of the Uva mountains, valley, rivers and my mother in her youthful days. Had he fathered other myths when he left us? I wonder what his cabin trunk contained? Clothes that had long gone out of fashion. Clothes he would never wear again, his khaki and drill suits wilting like the plumage of slain birds within that coffered trunk. Too late perhaps to take a white woman to wife. Too old. Too weary. Did he have a dream of fathering real children, not children like us, who had become mere figments of the imagination? Children who dwelt in that far away Prospero's island? He had given us over, oh so easily to others. First, the catechist, then the missionaries. But he had left us an annuity. His responsibility ceased there. Or so he thought, deluding himself.

Fatherhood. Motherhood. Sometimes I felt they merged so closely that the offspring of such a relationship could only be androgynous. At other times I felt that the ideas of parenting were poles apart. Distanced one from the other, my body stretched out to bridge that chasm. I would never know where the graves of my parents lay. That was not territory for me to claim. Enough of it had been taken over. Enough, enough. Let it all go back into that past, lost, irretrievable, remaining as a historical memory. Our names, Cathy's and mine, would never be engraved on those tombstones. My father's world, my mother's world, neither would know of our existence. I could not forget either of my parents. I had known them too well.

"Look at me, father, Alexander Laing, wearing clothes you never imagined I would wear – hatted and gloved, stockinged and perfectly shod, wearing a gown of beautiful cut. To be received and feted by Royalty! Not that we are any different as woman! Did you think that I would spend the rest of my life in a provincial town, never moving away from its circumscribed way of life while you sowed your wild oats, sought out adventure, ruled over thousands of acres of tea and rubber and then closed that chapter in your life, the final one, when you retired to your old life? We were never able to speak on equal terms. That is something I regret. But I can't deny you. No, I cannot. I followed you so tenaciously in my thoughts that I use your tongue in which to express my deepest feelings and to imagine yours. Guilt. Did you never feel guilty? That's an unanswered question. Perhaps this Garden Party will open even a slight aperture into my knowledge of where you belonged, your belief in the Empire, in hierarchies, in each of us occupying our separate niches." A sense of excitement filled me. I was ready to make my exploration.

My sister-in-law to be, Sophy and I, left for the Palace by 3.15 PM in a cab. The stream of cars, taxis, all bound for the same place was like a Chaucerian pilgrimage. We were held up in the traffic jam. Mounted police were all down the Mall. Yes, I felt a thrill of nervous excitation pass through me. Together with a sense of apprehension. There is always the thought of a welcome being withheld, of feeling forever, a stranger. An impersonal welcome. Eyes that do not see you but only attract the eye of the viewer. There are always people who need to be seen, to be admired, accorded respect, even adulation. But not ordinary beings like myself. My name will never be emblazoned on heraldic shields. I felt ... rebellious. What would I feel when I entered through those Palace gates? Ingrained in me since birth. Subservience. I had striven to that end, still not in sight, to reach my self-worth. The cock crowed three times. A warning. I would not let myself be easily betrayed.

I was a teacher. A respected teacher. I had acquired skill and fluency in my father's tongue. I acquired all the knowledge I could, through that exploration of his language. Yet, running through those deep, underground mines of my consciousness was also that other tongue, learned from my mother, glittering strands of precious ore. That was my secret knowledge. It contained a special music, rhythms to which my blood moved and danced, caught up in its swift current. I could share it if I chose to. If someone else had need of it. When I eventually married Edward, would I allow him to share those innermost secrets? I would have to wait and see. I would be marrying into a respected and well established Dutch Burgher family. Carry a name legitimized by society. Those people were proud of their genealogies. Bared all their secrets. Proudly. Yet engendered from conquest. Only separated through time, my father's and Edward's ancestors. I was a Eurasian – the term assigned to the breed to which I belonged. I sometimes felt as if I were severed into two different parts, my heart divided. Such were the thoughts that crowded my mind as we crawled in our cab through the melee of traffic.

After an eternity we reached the Palace Gates and walked

through them as if it were the most casual promenade we were taking in our lives. Yet we were considered privileged and honored guests. The invitation cards with their gold lettering and Royal insignia proved it. Sophy and I stepped confidently across the wide quandrangle. We then entered through open doors into a beautiful hall, the walls covered with paintings, statues on marble pedestals, gilt framed pictures, enormous porcelain vases embellished with Chinoiserie. The Empire followed us wherever we went. This was only the preliminary entrance to the Garden Party. We walked through the carpeted hallway to the place, hidden from the curious eyes of onlookers, into its very heart.

I had this feeling of belonging and not belonging. Summoned here, I was aware that it amounted to a kind of vassalage. We had to pay obeisance to those monarchs who were so alien to us, yet so deified through our historical imaginations. I too was to be a part of the tableau of the Empire. I was determined to have a pleasant afternoon, feeling the ambience of the place, weaving stories around the lives of the gathering around me. I wanted reality and not to be gazing at lithographs of royalty which hung on the walls of our missionary Home in Badulla. Who were these deified people? Were they too not flesh and blood showing the same loves and hates of human kind? Were we not all summoned here then with some purpose in mind? Loyal subjects who would not give way to rebellious thoughts, the invitation a reminder that we had vows of allegiance to fulfil. How long more would the mother country, whose surrogate children we were and to whom we paid so many eulogies, endure? To whose ever-replenished territorial bosom we went again and yet again, suckling for sustenance, all the while giving the raison d'être to that fertile and fecund body to thrive, to continue the role of nurturing us. I too fathered by that Empire but left alone and bereft by the man who was niggardly in true affection and who neglected his duty and responsibility. I had lost my true mother in the process. I was made to feel shame at being part of her. And shame generates guilt. This feeling of guilt sometimes gave me a sense of great malaise, an ache in my bones as if the marrow was being parched by a great fiery heat of longing. But these thoughts must be suppressed.

The missionaries had taught me that my true father dwelt in Heaven. Was that to be my compensation? The errant sheep would always be led back to the Shepherd of the Flock. What need then did I have of a weak and wandering, flesh and blood father? Let my mind be a sightseers map. I had the freedom to explore every monument, every landmark. I would leave, in my own way, an impress upon history. Make in-roads into forbidden territory. I would suckle the breast of all my surrogate mothers and take whatever solace I could to enable me to continue living, and in that act which gave me strength, vindicate that lost woman concealed in a village tucked away in the Uva valley whose funeral pyre I was never to view.

But why cast the slightest shadow on so perfect an afternoon? I couldn't help having these feelings. I had been subjected to too many years of submission, of accepting other peoples decisions, subscribing to their moral strictures. I had to acknowledge the fact of conquest in my own personal life and that was irksome. Here, at the Garden Party I was compelled to acknowledge that conquest symbolically, in the persons of Royalty but I had to bow my head to other kinds of conquest too. The island which had given me birth was subject to the power and domination of conquest, a bitter pill to swallow. At the same time, I had through my father, a stake in the Empire. An unacknowledged stake. Thus, there was both acceptance and rejection in my ambivalent and uneasy relationship with my adoptive parent, the mother country. The forbidden word, bastardization, the diminishing of legitimacy, the placing of the self outside the pale of society continually rankled. Sophy knew nothing of these thoughts. Her inheritance too had been through conquest, but those Dutch forebears of hers had legitimized their relationships in the Kirkhuis and their genealogies were contained in the Wapenherauts. Mine was a lonely journey.

I stood silently beside Sophy. She no doubt would have been

shocked by my thoughts. Heretical they were – I would not speak them out aloud. The band began to play the National Anthem. The strains were familiar to my ears. From the days of my childhood, I had heard and sung this anthem. There was no other anthem which belonged to the country where I was born. The anthem became a lullaby which lulled me into an unconscious slumber, shutting out all the other strains that emerged from the village, from the estate lines, the plaintive bamboo flute traveling at evening over the paddy fields and streams shrouded in a purple dusk. Drums from the Buddhist temple and from the Hindu kovil on the estate. Resonant. Staccato. Even at the cinema, we would all have to stand when the anthem was played. Acknowledging our suzerains, the King, the Queen of Great Britain. Our hands held straight at our sides. At attention. A stance that was often required of us at the morning drill. Attention. At ease. Ah, how we breathed a sigh of relief when the command was given, when we took up the more relaxed position. I felt myself once more standing straight, knees together, feet together. The habit was so ingrained within me. Following the old rules that had governed our lives but now, my unconscious act hidden, no longer singled out to be in the limelight, behind the crowds of guests in their afternoon gowns and fashionable hats, wide-brimmed or toques ... listening to those emotion – rousing strains, my lips fitting in the words silently, to each cadence.

> God save our gracious King
> Long live our noble King
> God save our King
> Send him victorious
> Happy and glorious
> Long to reign over us
> God save our King.

We could see nothing as yet with the crowds before us. What then was that revelation we were awaiting? I had been lost in my deepest reveries, oblivious of all the people around me. And now, here, in this place, this time, in this Garden I felt

I was back again in that childhood garden in the estate bungalow in Passara with its profusion of clove-scented carnations, phlox, gladioli and agapanthus lilies laid out in their ordered beds. Flowers tended and nurtured by the gardener, one of those migrant workers who had trekked from those distant ports of embarkation at Devipatanam or Paumben, taking the Northen Mannar Road to the upcountry estates. Those lawns mown so regularly, the bluegrass so smooth and evenly trimmed.

The Namunukula ranges of mountains towered before us. The bungalow where I had spent that brief, all too brief childhood, came back to my mind. Everything had bubble-vanished. With its loss, there was a greater loss, that of our childhood, Cathy's and mine. I was always searching for that lost garden in which my sister and I had played. Perhaps it was only a wilderness now, overgrown, untended, the ghostly footsteps of my father forever receding into the past, swallowed up by the towering jungles that surrounded it – kumbuk, ironwood, teak, satin, which had been cut down and cleared for the growing, first of coffee, then of tea. Perhaps once more, the wilderness and the forest had taken over with the belling of the sambhur echoing through those cloistered archways of dense and somber green, thick with leaf. There were leopards too in that wilderness, wild-boar rooting with their tusks in the undergrowth and herds of elephants that moved along their accustomed trails, delicately feeding off the tender green leaves.

Sophy nudged my elbow.

"Marian, you are dreaming. Wake up!"

I was back again in my senses, wearing my clever disguise, in my English clothes, looking "like one of them," yet in my heart of hearts, being separate, being different. Outwardly, there was nothing to tell me apart from the others. I had learned what to wear. Intuition too had helped. I wanted the best always. That was why I shopped in the most exclusive shops in London. In my island home the fashions that I saw were in the pages of Weldons Journals but here, in London, I could have the real thing.

Sophy was looking around her, at the throng of people milling around us, waiting for the curtain to rise. Something momentous had to happen to merit all the inspiration that had gone into this command performance. We had come to view Royalty, mingle not with patriots and revolutionaries but with loyal subjects of the Empire. To strengthen those special links which as yet showed no danger of weakening. Were those monarchs not to be regarded as human, like ourselves or did they still cling to the Divine Right of Kings where they felt that their special roles were God-ordained?

Who was I? And Sophy too? So mixed, so divided, both Sophy and myself, with our distinctive coloring, our historical, racial memories that hung miasmic over our consciousness. In the deepest recesses of our minds we could not forget the fact that we were children of conquest, albeit, at different periods. Our diversities were knit together by the common fact of our colonial inheritances. And now we belonged lock, stock and barrel to this Empire. The image we had been trained to acknowledge however, was the idealized one. The brutal facts of conquest, the wounds and mutilation of the psyche were the hidden ciphers in the documents of our baptismal records. We had, all these years, observed the power of throne and scepter governing our lives. I had observed, almost from the cradle, my father governing that conquered territory, the emissary and representative of that power. He too had made his fortune by being part of that great enterprise of colonialism which had exploited every avenue of the globe. The tea bushes on my father's estate were considered liquid gold. He shared in the wealth of the Empire. The destinies of all those Empire Builders were being shaped by an imperial architecture. What would history reveal of that construction? Pavilions, edifices official residences, were they all bubbles of the mind?

The anthem ended. The crowds parted and as if to satisfy our expectations, we found ourselves quite suddenly in the front row. Queen Elizabeth, dressed in black – Why? Was she in mourning? Accompanied by the two princesses. Princess Elizabeth and Princess Margaret Rose appeared before us. The

Queen bestowed a gracious smile upon us all. We could have touched her if only we had stretched our arms. But why have such a desire? To find out whether the Royals were real, human, not abstractions of an idea of that Imperial Power. My vision grew blurred. My mother ... where was she? I groped in my mind for that lost presence.

"We were really fortunate," Sophy whispered in my ear. "We saw them at such close quarters too."

"Did they see us?" I whispered.

Princess Margaret Rose had smiled. Princess Elizabeth had walked looking prim and proper. When all the excitement was over we stood on the outskirts of another crowd. Before long we found ourselves in the front row again, this time to view the stately and dignified Queen Mary dressed in a mauve gown. With her were the Princess Royal, Viscount Lascelles and the Duchess of Cornwall. I had the strangest feelings looking at their promenade through the Garden. Their view of the world would always be distanced from the common crowd as they rode in their carriages and in their Rolls Royces. They would be shielded from the terrible, shattering cataclysms of history until time, not revolutions, displaced them. Age. Death.

It was an historical viewing of all these Royal personages. They would never know how much their invisible presence was felt in our lives in that island of ours. Their duty done by their subjects on this occasion, they would depart from the scene and resume their royal roles. We would go back. Out into the unquiet and turbulent world.

There were other invitees present from the Ceylonese community in London. We met them while refreshments were being served. We introduced ourselves to each other – Lady Perez, Dewa Suriya Sena and wife, Mr. and Mrs. Gladwyn Perera and their daughters. Dewa Suriya Sena was one of the most famous of singers, a great composer and musician in our island. He looked elegant in his very individualistic attire, Jodhpur-style silk pants, a silk tunic and waistcoat. He and Lady Perez belonged to an elitist section of English educated Ceylonese society. Dewa Suriya Sena was equally at home with both western as well as oriental music. We became part of the group, happy to be together. "Ah, you young ladies are from Ceylon? On a visit to England? Holidaying here?" Deva Suriya Sena inquired. They were charmingly curious about Sophy and myself. We would never meet once we returned home. We moved in different social circles. We did not share in the prerogatives of wealth and power. Here, as strangers we forged whatever bond we could find to keep us together, so as not to feel outsiders. To create our own welcome. "Well," I said, "I am at the Institute of Education at the University of London."

"And how have you been spending your time in the city? Your first trip here, isn't it? Fortunate to been invited to the Garden Party." Dewa Suriya Sena murmured between bites of paper-thin sandwiches and iced millefleurs. I sipped hot tea. I found it fragrant. Was it a blend of Ceylon teas? Broken Orange Pekoe or Darjeeling?

Sophy was talking to Lady Perez who was draped in the elegant folds of a French chiffon sari with sprays of flowers – mignonettes I think – painted on it. In her ears she wore dangling earrings of pearls set in gold. Encircling her throat were three strands of pearls. She and her husband enjoyed those titles bestowed on them as loyal subjects of the Empire. Within our society, hierarchies were established by those honorable titles. Lady and Sir. Were they not separate then from the rest of their people. Did those titles not stand for compliance to an alien rule?

Lady Perez turned to me "What are your plans for the future?" she asked me.

"We're looking forward, Sophy and I, to touring the continent. We're anxious, however, because of all the rumors of war."

"Yes, war clouds seem to be threatening, aren't they? What a tragedy that would be – a Second World War – we hope the crisis can be averted. Ceylon too will be affected like the rest of the colonies. Well, Miss Laing, what do you feel?"

"Well, if it is a war in which Great Britain will be involved, our country will be inevitably drawn in. We're part of the Empire.... Our allegiance will be unquestioning...."

"Let us hope there will be an opportunity of meeting again when we are back home," Deva Suriya Sena murmured.

"I would like to hear you sing," I said. "Perhaps I will attend one of your concerts in Colombo." We smiled and parted, mingling with the rest of the guests. We made friends with another couple – Mr. and Mrs. Copp from Canada. Sophy and I walked round the Palace Gardens with them then back to the gates, through the hall (sat in one of the chairs this time) chatted to a policeman who wanted us to go back and sign the Book. Our names would always be there, a whole page preserved for a posterity who would think of us all as anonymous people.

Other dignitaries compelled our attention – the Lord Chamberlain and the Financial Secretary. We met Lady Fisher Smith, crippled owing to an accident but she was charming.

What did I wish for at this moment? Perhaps that I could walk towards that man who had been my father. But he had turned away a long time ago. I could only retrieve that memory that he had once been in my life. I wished that we could have walked together along so many paths ... with my mother's presence too besides us ... a presence that he acknowledged, not one that was both silent and invisible....

My father had made his lasting behest. I would not allow that bonding of parenthood to go unacknowledged. Its denial would be nullification of an identity I constructed as I continued my journey.

OF LOVE AND LONELINESS

It is never too late to speak of that love for someone who is no longer alive. No, never. She shared her secret with me one evening when I was a child stepping across the boundaries that separated her adult world from mine. She opened the door of that secret room where all discoveries are made. I entered and those moments are there, forever embedded in my mind.

There is not a single photograph left behind of her, my adopted Godmother. I tried after all these long years to trace at least one that could be in the possession of her nieces who had emigrated to Australia years before but nothing had been preserved. Only the memory of that gentle face, that soft maternal body remains. Aunty Gladys. She belonged to my childhood living in that large rambling old house, Royden, with the two jambu trees standing in the front garden. The back garden was a place of endless fascination and mystery to me. The entire slope behind the house was made up of terraced flower beds with winding paths that led downwards to paddy fields beyond which lay the railway lines. It was at Royden that my memories of Aunty Gladys and Uncle Alroy began.

Royden was a house which to me was full of sunlight flooding in from the open windows to fall on the cretonne upholstered furniture and the carpets covering the wood paneled floors of the drawing room. A house that was always filled with people, the young nieces, Sylvia and Thelma and the nephew Noel, the uncles and aunts, friends. It was never a lonely house filled with silence and shadows. Even now, years later I dream of houses, different houses in different landscapes. The houses, some of which belong to the reality of that era we lived in, in the provincial town of Kadugannawa.

Royden. Paradise View. Houses with names where people settled in to create the history of their lives. Before death and migration changed everything and people moved away from what I realized would never be permanent safe enclaves. In each of those houses there was festivity and celebration. I was yet to know violence, death or loss in any of them. The adult world appeared to be safe. But it was a world from which I often strayed, wanting to listen to the silence of my own thoughts, to explore my own dreams.

I was emerging out of the chrysalis. I was becoming more aware of that adult world which admitted us as children to share in those elaborate and ritualistic games which were performed as part of a way of life. There existed a kind of formal pattern which the adults followed and into which we were initiated. There were dance steps to be learned. There were gameboards with rules. We danced the Palais Glide and the Lambert Walk. We clowned and bumped about with Boomps-a-daisy and Roll-out-the-Barrel. Foxtrots. Quicksteps. Tangos. Rhumbas. Waltzes. The music came from HMV gramophones, pianos, guitars. We spent hours playing Thiamchonal. We learned of reaching a destination, of meeting hazards on the way, of having to start all over again on that gameboard. We treated victory, a heady sensation, with joy and faced defeat without rancor. As we danced and sang, the rhythms of life entered our blood, the preamble to the mating dance at which the adults were so adept.

Where then was Aunty Gladys? In those early days? She was always there. Her hair smoothly brushed back over her forehead, a deep wave held back by a tortoiseshell slide, wearing dresses of silk or linen, with collars, buttons down front, a buckled belt, court shoes, stockings and with that air of ineffable kindness.

She had no children of her own but I never felt their absence. Her life was filled with Sylvia, with Thelma, with

Noel, with all of us. I followed her about when we went to Royden for all those lunches, dinners, parties. She showed me how she made her own ginger beer in big earthenware crocks floating with fat plums. Ice cream churns were filled with custard, the wooden barrels packed with ice and the handle turned steadily until the ice cream formed. She showed me how to make pastellas, the pastry rolled out and cut in circles, the patty curry spooned in the center. I would fold the pastry, press down the edges, seal them with egg white and make fluted serrations with a fork. It was at some of those parties that I learned of the trickster pastella. Filled with mysterious fillings, if you were caught you would have to let go of all shyness and inhibitions and sing, dance or perform antics to amuse the others.

Royden was a world in itself, of entertainment, hospitality, friendship. Sylvia and Thelma played duets on the piano, strummed on Hawaiian guitars, sang alto and soprano, voices harmonizing, blending so beautifully together as they sang those sentimental romantic songs, "Harbour Lights," "When My Dreamboat Comes Home," "Blue Hawaii," "On the Beach of Waikiki." Where were those far away places, islands and azure blue oceans, those idyllic landscapes? That map of the world was still to be shaped in my mind. This small provincial world contained the only life I knew. My aunts, my father's sisters, placed a globe on the dining table and set it spinning to show us where the Cunard liners would take them on their voyages to England and Europe. Those worlds were unknown places to me. As Sylvia and Thelma swayed their hips and danced, I danced with them too. We followed those mimic steps wearing full bunched skirts with floating streamers and leis of frangipani about our necks.

After the piano duets, the singing accompaniment and Hawaiian dancing, we children were summoned to an early dinner. We sat with our chairs drawn up to the dining table like adults but with starched white damask serviettes tucked around our necks. As we grew older, the serviettes were placed on our laps. The dining table was spread with damask linen, cones of snowy serviettes standing upright beside our plates, gleaming silver cutlery and cut glass tumblers. The glass water jug was always covered with a circle of tasseled net bordered with tiny loops and tinkling colored beads. We ate the same food as the adults, the dinners being formal ones. There was the spinning of yarn after yarn, the men emptying their brimming glasses of whiskey while the ladies sipped sweet sherry. Music entered our psyches with those dulcet voices of Sylvia and Thelma drifting through the still air. One day those metaphors of dreamboats, harbor lights and blue Hawaii would change and take on a new reality through the passage of those migrations to the Antipodes. But all that would take years to be accomplished. Until then, here was a moment encapsulated in time as we sat sedately, tilting our soup spoons half-filled with consommé delicately away from the soup plate without spilling a drop in its passage, inclining our heads ever so slightly as if to receive a benediction. Grilled seer fish followed. Roast chicken, boiled potatoes, Heinsz greenpeas, a salad of crisp lettuce and tomatoes in vinaigrette. A dessert of caramel pudding or stewed fruit, apples, pears, peaches, apricots with custard and a quivering red moss-jelly. And so we ate, sitting sedately like grownups. Going through those early menus of life.

I suddenly became conscious that time was passing. The dinner parties at Royden were coming to an end. Uncle Henny died and only Thelma and her mother were left behind at Paradise View. Without Uncle Henny, Paradise View became lonely. The widow's face grew sad. She rarely smiled. That view of an imagined Paradise became an illusory glimpse of a transient world. I, the little girl who had stood beneath the jambu tree calling out to Uncle Henny, was now growing up. We too had to leave our bungalow perched on the hill and move to the township of Kandy. Uncle Alroy and Aunty Gladys sold Royden to the widow of a Professor of Botany from the University of Colombo. She and her son took up their abode in that house with the jambu trees and terraced garden. The willow pattern plates that covered the dining room walls were carefully taken down and put away. The furniture, the piano, the guitars were packed away. Uncle Alroy and Aunty Gladys became our close neighbors in Kandy. They lived in a house called Inbastan. They always lived in houses that had names. This house had a small courtyard with a little gate that opened out onto the main road. Our house just a few doors away had a parapet wall with potted palms, an allspice tree and the deadly nightshade plant where I used to watch the insects drawn into that lethal viscous fluid struggling, drowning. There was also a flourishing margosa tree. Swinging plants swung from the eaves in hollowed-out bamboo and the little garden was full of squirrels and birds.

Once more the visits were interchanged between our families and the pianos in both our houses were heard again with the singsongs and duets continuing. There were fancy dress parties and birthday parties. We were in an out of each others houses. I was no longer the child I was and measuring my height against the wall I found I was growing taller. My view of the world was now an all embracing one. Aunty Gladys was still so much a part of my life. The parties continued. The dance of life whirled unabated. New people entered our lives. New friends. The tempo of the dance began to change. New words, new sentiments, new melodies. The rhythm of our lives became more frenetic.

The Second World War was at its height. British soldiers and sailors were the new entrants at the parties. Our spirits were readying themselves for a new migration. For parting. For departure. For farewells and that going away from which there would be no return. Condemned, each of us, to the eternal loneliness of the spirit.

As I reached adolescence, I began to retreat into a shell, absorbed in that world of books which spoke of emotions I was still to experience. Walking alone on deserted roads searching for the irretrievable landscape of that childhood I had left behind in Kadugannawa. Searching for that revelatory glimpse which would give me knowledge of myself. My solitary walks often took me along Halloluwa Road where there was a dark bat-infested tunnel, from which fetid odors emanated. Water seeped down the drip ledges on the sides of the hollowed out rock walls. The dense darkness which did not admit a single ray of light but which was filled with a secret life of its own was a place of fear and mystery. It was a tunnel which belonged to history, the rock blasted by prisoners of war during the colonial era of British rule. Its purpose, a shorter diversionary route for military purposes. Soon it fell into disuse. Abandoned to humans but a different kind of life flourished within that moisture-laden air. The odor of a forgotten prehistoric life which engulfed the senses. Within, there were myriads of insects, reptiles, bats, rank vegetation where from the detritus of buried seed new roots snaked forth, new plants sprang up. I was often drawn to that cave mouth but it was forbidden territory. There were boundaries but what did I know of danger or fear at that point of my life? I was however aware of the hidden force of darkness. I did not explore that tunnel but walked through sunlight and climbed innumerable steps to reach the summit of the hill above the tunnel.

Up there in the silence of shadowy trees and huge clumps of fern, the outside world appeared to be the safer world, the sunlight filtering through the leaves deceptively mitigating the darkness of that subterranean tunnel. I could not even explain to myself why I wanted to be solitary and alone on that deserted road. My untried innocence, the loss of which was inevitable, protected those few years from ambush and from violation of body and mind. No one could protect me when I stepped into that cave. The darkness of my own inner thoughts swallowed me up and then spewed me out to scatter in fragments at the mouth of the dark tunnel.

One evening when I walked into Inbastan alone, I encountered Aunty Gladys. The others were in some other part of the house. Inbastan was one of those old houses that stretched along a passage with a maze of rooms on one side. It also had an inner courtyard and steps leading into unknown places with a wall and a door that shut out the outer world.

The house began on the main upper road and then fell onto the lower road. Each room was enfolded in its own privacy.

"Come, Lynette," Aunty Gladys called me softly. "There is something I want to show you. Come, let's go into our bedroom." She led me gently by the hand. I followed her. It was the first time I was to enter her bedroom. And the last. The bedroom with glass paned windows which opened out onto the inner courtyard was arranged in a predictable way. There was no riddle for me to puzzle out in the way the solid teak furniture occupied all the habitual places. The twin beds, side by side was part of the accepted intimacy of a staid and established marriage. It was a sharing of that bond that welded two souls together with invisible bands of steel which nothing would break. There stood the mirrored dressing table, the massive wardrobe, the bedside table, a chair or two. The furniture displayed nothing of the turmoil of tumultuous thoughts and feelings. At night the bedspreads would be neatly folded and put away and Uncle Alroy would wear his pyjamas, Aunty Gladys, her nightgown. They would say their prayers and sleep, clasped perhaps in that warm embrace of a long tried and unaltered or unalterable relationship.

I sat on the edge of the bed careful not to ruffle the bedspread. Aunty Gladys went up to the wardrobe, opened its locked doors with a silver key from a bunch of keys of various sizes and lifted from the top shelf a big, beautiful life-sized baby doll.

It is only now, many years later, when I have given birth to my own children and cradled them in my arms looking into their unshadowed eyes to see myself as I had once been that I realize the longing Aunty Gladys must have had to share her secret. It was a secret that could be shared only with one such as myself, who had known her all those long years. Woman. Child. Child. Woman. Each of us had to step delicately over that invisible line which separated the years of our lives. For me, the adult experience was still nebulous. What did I know or understand of that aching void, that hankering to feel the throb and heartbeat of a living child in that birthing. In the cradling arms of Aunty Gladys and myself lay a real, living, breathing child. I held that baby in my arms and within myself I felt the stirrings of a strange new love. It was a love that reached me from that lonely heart. How many years was it since she had created this child of her imagination? How many years was it since she had hidden that child of her imagination away, ... away from prying eyes ... preparing with patient and loving care, the layette for the baby. The smocked baby shirts, the knitted bonnets and booties. The baby linen delicately embroidered. How many years had it taken her to share this secret with any living soul? I became selfish all of a sudden. I wanted to take that baby home. I wanted to possess her. I had longed for another baby brother or baby sister. Unfulfilled longings. I could not ask Aunty Gladys outright. Some delicacy of feeling prevented me but I made up my mind that I would make my mother the go-between. The negotiator. When I did tell my mother she refused my pleading request. She understood Aunty Gladys. She was a sensitive woman. I let it rest. I never mentioned the baby doll to Aunty Gladys again nor was I ever invited to hold or bathe or wipe with soft linen that doll. Nor would I dust the body with talcum powder sprinkled on the swansdown power puff. Once only, once. Never again. Those exquisite hand-sewn garments were folded and put away. We had entered that inner room, a space in time where no clocks marked the passing years, no pendulum struck its resonant chords. Silence. The closing of the door. The sharing of that secret which up to this day fills me with a sense of sadness.

I still remember the formal patterns, the landscaping of that childhood garden with the two jambu trees covered with clusters of deep red jambus. The laden branches were filled with birds and squirrels. I had stood beneath those trees and looked out beyond the garden onto the road calling out to those who were inside the house – "I can see Uncle Henny. I can see Uncle Henny." How brief was that glimpse of him. How lost that glimpse of Paradise View. The landscape changed and we all went away. The jambu trees remained until they grew old and gnarled and the fruits grew tart and shrunken.

Aunty Gladys was part of that going away. She was with me until a while longer, remaining long enough to extend my knowledge of life and the world. At the same time she left me with a sense of deep guilt. I never had the courage to make my own confession to her. And now to whom can I make that confession to ease the pain in my memory? Only to the ghost of remembrance.

Even to this day I am racked with guilt and sorrow. Being childless, both Uncle Alroy and Aunty Gladys lavished their love on their beautiful golden retriever. One evening rushing into their house with my parents on one of our evening visits, I who was the last to enter, left the wooden gate carelessly open in my eagerness to go inside. The dog ran out onto the main road. She was knocked down by a passing car. The body was brought indoors and Aunty Gladys wept uncontrollably. Her tears fell as she stroked the limp form that had ceased to breathe. I could not bear to see her cry. I could not confess those words that may have altered her love for me. It would have destroyed me. It would have destroyed her. Would she have ever forgiven me for that loss?

It is only now I make my confession. It is only now that I understand that there are vast dark spaces in our lives, locked rooms within ourselves that no one enters. Only now I understand what it is to cause hurt to those whom we love and to those whom we cannot bear to lose.

Forgive me. I am to blame. I left the door open. I watched you weep. I lacked the courage to tell you that I had been thoughtless. Careless. Unthinking.

Was it cowardice that led me to save myself from your hurt? I did not want to lose that love which made you trust me. I could not betray myself. I could not betray what you had taught me. And so I remained silent until I lost my fear of the truth.

THE WITNESS

On the 2nd March 1815 the sovereign rights of the last politically independent remnant of the Sinhalese people were irrevocably surrendered to the English Crown by the adigars, disawas and other chiefs claiming to act on behalf of the inhabitants.

– A History of Ceylon under British Rule,
Father S. G. Perera

The temperature of Kandy is believed to have increased in warmth since the surfaces of the surrounding mountains have been dried by the felling of trees, to convert the forests into plantations of coffee – and it is certainly remarkable that although grapes will not ripen there now as the vine requires a winter repose, wine from the grapes grown on the spot was produced by the Dutch. Spilberg, who drank of it in 1602, describes its quality as excellent and Valentyn at a later period speaks of it in similar terms.

– Ceylon (Vol. II),
Sir James Emerson Tennent

Had I seen it all then long before it happened. Or was it after it had happened. As in a dream. Relived the whole experience. Was I in that room where those two old sisters had been fast asleep in their beds when one of them had been strangled to death. Left there until that morning when her body was discovered. The other grievously hurt. Death. Sleep.

Hardly distinguishable. The two of them Harriet and Caroline in their white Victorian nightgowns with lace and pin tucks. All my life I have been haunted by my own memories. The two sisters left behind their ghosts that still wander through my imagination, their presence seeming to compel me to write, to record what I remember of them. Childhood has its ghosts. The belief in that alternative reality that exists beyond the mundane world with adult pressures and sanctions imposed upon its freedom. There were no boundaries in the world of my imagination.

Valleys and hills merged into a peerless sky with no brushstrokes to separate or divide the world. There was no dichotomy in that landscape. Time had no laws. Only daylight and dark. Flowers opened out like poems. It was only later that the discovery of the flies, the insects entrapped in the viscous fluid of the deadly nightshade, were discovered. Too late for rescue. The early preoccupation with death began there in that discovery, listening to fairy tales that enchanted you with magic and sorcery. The entrance to a hidden world which contained the greater truths of good and evil. Knowledge could not be denied.

The two sisters whom I encountered early in life gave me glimpses and insights into a world other than my own although I never spoke to them, only observed and listened to their voices on those evening walks on the bund of the Kandy Lake. My mother described the yachts that sailed in the regattas. Once even a powder magazine was housed on the island in the middle of the lake. Now a few trees and bushes had sprung up there.

During those childhood walks I first encountered voices that were different to mine and at the same time akin. I could understand the words they spoke, listen to the innocent prattling of the two sisters as they alighted from the car with their brother, taking a few steps in a curve of the bund, pausing, looking out on the gentle ripple of water shaded by green overhanging branches thickly leaved, on the sanctuary of Udawattekele, on blue ranges of hills and the Dalada Maligawa, the Temple of the Tooth.

What have I been questioning all these years and why have I never forgotten them. Perhaps it is not so much that death which at that time filled me with a sense of shock and horror but the beginnings of my own loss of innocence through knowledge that the garden of Eden was not the paradisal myth we could walk in forever. It was in that garden that we encountered each other. They passed me by, the two sisters but I paused to watch and to observe them minutely. Their fragile, slightly humpbacked bodies, flower stalks bent in too strong winds, high necked, long sleeved, ankle length gowns with sprigs of tiny flowers, cameo brooches and smooth grey-brown hair coiled, braided and fastened with tortoiseshell combs. They belonged to a different generation, had not relinquished that period of time belonging to the past. They would for all times embody the spirit of an empire which they had adopted to become their own. They belonged, looking back, to my own historical vision of this township which had all the signs of that usurpation. The churches, the missionary schools and colleges, the big colonial shops, the hotel, the colonial architecture of the houses that clustered on one side of the lake. And even the naming of the roads and streets and carriage road. A map of historical routes. The names of those British Empire Builders, Governors and their wives. Brownrigg Street, Ward Street, Torrington Square, Lady Blake's Drive, Lady Horton's Drive. The park above the lake with its fountain and flowering plants. Wace Park. Plants that were introduced by the colonial botanists. Summer houses like the pavilions in the gardens of the great English Country Houses. Mazes. Gazebos.

In the very heart of the city at the foot of the sanctuary for flora and fauna stood the Governor's House, the King's Pavilion with its landscaped garden, rare trees and plants.

Looking back after all these years the lives of those two sisters, even the violent death of one of them, are seen against that colonial backdrop where carriage roads encircled the hills, where new styles of architecture had been introduced and new varieties of plants and trees brought from other colonies, from different parts of the world, to grow and flourish in that paradisal garden. Together with the indigenous trees and the overwhelming luxuriance of natural vegetation which nothing could stifle. All that was foreign, fruits and spices, all that was exotic, intermingled in the parks and gardens. The Garden of Eden was colonized to bring wealth to all who had knowledge of those sources. To me, reviewing that past, those eras cannot yield the simple facts of life and death in any other context than as that of seeing murder as an act of rebellion against that Colonial Order. For me, as a child, the garden was an unspoilt place until sin, synonymous with knowledge, entered. To me then, in my childhood, the reptile was representative of dark and evil forces. Temptation analogous to guilt. I would be the eternal penitent in my pilgrimage. I could never escape from the guilt of the great temptations that the Eden Garden was so full of. There was no other way to appease my hunger and thirst except by satisfying the desire to taste the fruit of knowledge.

I had felt as a child, more than a sense of curiosity about the lives of those sisters and their brother in that almost forgotten era. All of us belonged to that colonial backdrop. We accepted the changing landscape of those times. I was not aware then of that unnamed man whose face I was never to see, concealed in the shadows. The revelatory moment came together with realization. Our lives were curbed and trammeled by historical forces. I too had lived within the shadow of the subjugator. I could not accept my own innocence, the innocence lost through knowledge. That act of murder had been symbolic. I was the witness to that rebellion. I had to find my freedom in different ways.

Going back to the past. Taken for long walks round the Kandy lake, as a child. Walks beneath the tall, shady trees with wide spreading branches. Pausing to feed the fish and tortoises that rose to the surface when I scattered puffed corn on the green ripples of the lake waters. I would see them, the two old ladies, on those evening walks with my elder sister and my cousin Diana holding the hand of Diana's nanny. Diana had come with her parents on a holiday to Kandy – her father was working for a British Firm in India. They had brought the nanny all the way from there. An English-speaking nanny in starched white muslin sari. We were all staying at the same boarding house run by my mother's friend, Miss Thomas – Aunty Tommy.

I was curious about the people I saw on the bund of the lake. I would never cease to wonder how deep its waters were. Imagined myself on that little island in the middle of the lake. How cool the breezes were that blew across the water bearing that slightly fishy smell. Listening to snatches of conversation of those who sat on those wrought-iron seats waiting for the dusk to fall. Some of my first journeys into the outer world. All unaware of age and death. Or even birth. A timeless age of childhood. A world which had no dimensions, no perspectives. Boundaries did not exist to hinder the mind's exploration. The image of the two old ladies was part of that landscape. I would never forget them. Time became the spider weaving its patient web, watching with avid intent the minute gossamer-winged fly. The backdrop to that tranquil scene, the forest sanctuary to me then, was an imagined world. Later to become a place of violence, death, and horror. Murder.

I asked my mother about the two old ladies I saw that evening. They wore long gowns of grey-blue figured silk with lace collars, white stockings and buckled shoes. The fashion they followed belonged to a bygone era. The early years of the century. Every strand of smoothly brushed hair in place. Accompanied by a single, middle-aged male, who I was to learn later, was their unmarried brother. The sisters were spinsters. The Miss Bevans, I was told. My mother knew who they were but we never went on visits to their home to drink tea from transparent cups of fine bone china and to nibble Assorted Peak Freens biscuits. Golden Puffs. My favorite biscuits. The two sisters, delicate, frail shoulders swathed in tasseled woolen shawls, their voices like those cries of birds that drifted over the lake from the hidden depth of leafy cages. My childhood was full of secrets. Children always have secrets. Keeping them through the years.

The sisters and the brother did not observe my scrutiny as they alighted from the shining black Ford car driven by a chauffeur. There was innocence in my scrutiny. An uncorrupted gaze I did not know then that one day I would lift those characters out of the past and place them on these pages that I print from memory. They mingle with the other characters that slowly emerge from that chiaroscuro of images of which I too was a part. I was not allowed to forget them. They are part of the haunting of my childhood. The ghosts that still lurk in the shadows. The gentle ghosts of memory.

I gradually began to insert myself into the past. It took me years and years. I asked questions of people who may have remembered the murder case and the trial but then memories were fading with age and time. I began to keep notes on my own investigations traveling through time on a different plane of reality. I had observed the old ladies with a child's vision. I created secret fictions. No one was aware that I was observing that strange menage alighting on the bund from that old Ford car. A car which looked more like a black carriage. A hearse. I watched them carefully. I was never to forget them.

On our walks we would pass the old colonial house that they had lived in with its wide verandahs, thick-girthed pillars and tiled roof. The well-kept lawns, the garden and behind it the densely forested sanctuary for flora and fauna. A house with its colonial architecture designed for the tropics. A landmark on the historical map.

These were the houses bordering the lake, that the British government officials had once occupied. They had been the government agents and the civil engineers – the British bureaucracy. The houses so minutely described in books written by colonial historians. Pages filled with details of the colonial architecture designed for its adaptability to the tropics with wide, columned verandahs, spacious high-ceilinged rooms, windows and doors with their jalousies to let in the breeze, tiled and cemented floors. There were wine cellars, storerooms, servants quarters, outhouses, stables. The walls were whitewashed with chunam, the roofs tiled. The rooms were filled with ornately carved Dutch and Indo-Portuguese furniture of ebony, satinwood, calamander, jak. The gardens were a delight to the colonial botanists with the flowering plants and trees that grew naturally in the island, the fruit trees and vines and the new breeds, the new seeds, the hybrids introduced from the other British colonies adapting and acclimatizing themselves to their new environment. The colonial garden where the native plants flourished together with the hybrid. Given a new Latin nomenclature, the myths embodied in them revealed in translation. These houses, these gardens were now a distinct feature of a landscape transformed into something historical with eras and epochs demarcated as in the ordered flower beds.

The house in which the Bevan family lived was one of those historical nineteenth century edifices. All unconscious at that early age, without an awareness of the transformations in the native landscape, of history, I was looking at a monument that would not endure for much longer. Time would scrawl its graffiti in the cracked plaster, with the inroads of familiar termites, vestiges of clinging ivy and memories woven like gossamer threads of chrysalides and webs. The spider generations would live on and the house itself be one day covered with festoons of webs that screened off the past. A past to which I had once been witness. A past in which I too had had a stake but which I had been able to escape from. At that time there was one other, that gardener in the Bevan family who had tried to escape from the subjugation of that history. His escape, as I now see it after all these years, was a desperate act of rebellion against that Empire which he felt had taken away his heritage. There was no other way he could reclaim it other than through his act of breaking into the domain of the inner rooms, of trying to retrieve in some past what had once belonged to his people, the myth of treasure which had the power to give him his freedom. Everything around him was part of that subjugation. His will was trammeled by the throttling growth of the plants which stifled his very breath. Nothing belonged to him any longer unless he retrieved a little part at least of that treasure in the hands of those who were representatives of that imperial power. One night he entered the house, the room of the two sisters. That was the night of that death. Those who woke up the next morning found the room in violent disarray, the contents of the huge wardrobe spilling out of drawers and shelves, one of the sisters barely conscious.

I am now the only witness to that hitherto unwritten, unrecorded episode in history.

One of the sisters was strangled to death. The other bruised and hurt but still breathing. Brother and sister were left to live out their lonely lives in that house by the lake.

The assailant? My mother told me later on who had been under suspicion for death and the attack, but not his name. He vanished. No one knows what became of him.

I am now the only living witness to that hitherto unwritten, unrecorded episode in the history of that colonial township. I want to preserve the histories of women, nameless now to history but who are still alive in memory. Women – frail, vulnerable, nurtured in those eras. The young girl raped and murdered in the wilderness of Bible Rock on a Sunday school picnic. That lone, lost cry which no one heard. "She was a loner. She lagged behind." I once wrote to the priest who had been the leader of that picnic beseeching him to remember but there was no answer to that letter. Was I violating his peace of mind, disturbing what he desired to forget? Was there no expiation for his guilt at forgetting the lost sheep? And that young poet – a young woman who had been gagged, strangled, her body shoved into a cupboard in that old family house. That act of violence perpetrated by the men who had come to clear the wilderness of her garden. The doors locked in on her. Her poems her only living memory.

Yes, I want to preserve the memories of women who had lived and breathed and died violently. Women who had walked so freely in their gardens of Eden and died before their time. Gardens. Old houses. I remember that garden many years later in those acres of a country house in the South West of England. At Exeter. I was walking through historical eras there. It was a garden that was a colonized world. There was a stone carving of pineapples, in one corner the remains of a tropical garden seen in its full splendor with a description in a nineteenth century page of country life framed behind glass and the Italian garden with its stone sculpture of a woman.

So, starting out from that old house with its colonial styled architecture specially designed for the tropics with wide verandahs and that garden with all the exotics the two sisters had lived, they themselves hybrid blooms that had emerged out of conquest. But these were thoughts, ideas that emerged out of the memories of the past – of childhood – in that far away era. I had to make connections through my investigations.

THE GARDENER

The two sisters were like hothouse blooms that grew into rare exotics among the flowering creepers of bigonias, ipomoeas, and the conventional flowers in their garden. Their petals were muted. Velvety soft like old camphor-scented silk. Flowers that were supported on stalks twisted and bent by invisible storms. While Harriet and Caroline lived out their innocent lives within the house, the gardener spent hour after hour, day after day, digging up the flowerbeds and planting rose slips, grafting new varieties of rose blooms, cutting, pruning, snipping off the wilting and withering plants and flowers. He had come to this house a young man from a Kandyan village in the Dumbara valley, laying out flowerbeds, landscaping the garden like the gardens of the British officials who lived in the environs of the lake. Houses similar to the one in which the Bevan family lived, the architecture so different to the houses of the Kandyan chieftains with their carved pillars and inner courtyards. Houses built, flower beds and lawns carefully laid out where once the jungle had been.

He was the creator of this garden but while he planted dahlias amid barbeton daisies, canna lilies, roses and gladioli, the wild orchids and tiger lilies, the sunset-spread of lantana, the white trumpet-shaped poisonous datura sprang up among the ferns and mosses that spilled over from the sanctuary behind the house. There were flaring green leaves shaped like cobra hoods in old temple murals and twisting lianas swinging like cables from free branches. Blossoms of Queen of the Night inundated the garden with an over-powering fragrance making the senses swoon in the dusk. The garden was an orchard too with nutmeg, guavas, avocados, mangoes. There were passion fruit vines and loquats, granadillas, sour sop. From where had all these strange seeds fallen, to root themselves in this rich earth?

Beyond the boundaries of this garden there was no other life for him. The gardener seldom or never went back to his village any longer and as he grew older he wondered whether he could ever escape from that web of flowerbeds that ensnared his every thought. This was the only world he was expected to live in, watching the plants and flowers bloom and die according to their seasons of growing. The sanctuary loomed over the house bordering the lake. Within it the ancient trees were allowed to grow, trees that he could not name, but were there from the beginning of time. Deep within the thickly growing trees were the tribes of monkeys, leopard, reptiles. There were caves where hermits lived and deep pools of water. It was a world protected for the fauna and flora that belonged to primeval nature. The way of life he had given up in that Kandyan village with its chequered green paddy fields and winding river. Thoughts of that part of his life awoke memories of what he had left far behind him when he heard the echoes of drum and horanewa from the Dalada Maligawa. Nothing could change those memories.

Where could he have had a kinder master, less demanding mistresses and the assurance that he would have a home here for the rest of his life yet how long more would he have to serve them. He watched them all grow older and older while his plants were full of sap and there was that perpetual renewal in the growing, the blooming, the putting forth of the fruit and flower, their withering and dying. The other servants were content with their lot but within himself the gardener began to feel a sense of unease, of unhappiness. Barebodied he worked among the barbetons, the roses, the gladioli and Holy Ghost orchids. He felt himself resembling a plant thriving in the sun and heavy showers of rain. He tended the garden with so much care, gathering the ripe passion fruit and plucking the mangoes that grew on the overhanging branches. Many of the ripe fruit had fallen half-eaten by bats and squirrels. No children came into the garden. Yes, here the only marauders were the birds, the squirrels and the wonderoo monkeys that came to pillage the fruit.

He felt himself growing older. How much longer would this family (and they were already old) live? Where would he go after their death? Who would look after him in his old age. He lived on the fringe of other people's lives. His nature that had grown with the plants began to change. To grow twisted and serpentine, the strong vine of his body clinging to the tree torsos. Choking and feeding off the parent tree. Away from his plants at night he began to weave dreams. The fireflies spread a fine mesh of glittering light over every bush and as he gazed on those myriad sparkling stars, he waited for some kind of revelation. It would come, he knew it would come or he would die soon, buried in the orchard, forgotten. He felt the presence of the wild leopard in the sanctuary. The whirring of insects sweeping down with the wind. He would, he must escape. He had been displaced from the village in the valley with its familiar landscape for long enough.

He began to feel a kind of terror grow within him. Rooted in the earth he would resemble the gnarled ancient araliya trees or lie like a forgotten bulb growing hard, unwatered beneath. Never to emerge into the light. He had a name which was seldom used in this household. The name that he brought with him from the village. A name that belonged to ancient kings and chieftains but here it was forgotten. When he was alone he had to remind himself of his real name. The name given him here was that of a king who lived thousands of miles away. A name which belonged to those officials who ruled the land. It was not his true name.

He waited for that promised revelation. The fireflies that sparkled in the bushes illumined the path that led down from the sanctuary. One night the leopard came down to the garden. And the next night too. He told no one about the leopard. It was a small leopard. He felt no fear of it. And it always went back to the sanctuary. That was where it belonged.

It was then that he decided he must finally go. He would first escape into the forest sanctuary. No one would search for him there. The wilderness was impenetrable. There were caves where he could shelter. He began to plan his route. Strategies formed in his mind. He was patient. The months passed. The flowers shattered the air with their brilliance. The garden was a conflagration of color with bright red pom-pom lilies, blood-red barbetons, dark blue-red dahlias. Within his veins the blood grew heated, the need to escape more urgent. Let nature take over the garden, the plants grow rampant. The air was thick with pollen and flying grass seeds. The snail, the caterpillar, the grub, the worm, the chameleons and bloodsuckers took over the garden. It was their natural territory.

Let the wilderness tangle into snares and the dead leaves pile up, beneath the fresh green ones. He would not be there to curb and trammel nature. To prune and trim the lawns. He felt excluded from the life within the old colonial house. He felt the intensity of his dispossession. To him that old structure was one of power, but he had no share in it. What he planned to do was to enter into that house and take, in some small part, the wealth that he felt had been stolen from him and from his people. He was alone in this act of rebellion. Once he entered the house he would take whatever he felt rightfully belonged to him, not the foreign bank notes. There were other things. He felt that if he possessed those gold sovereigns with their impress of the king then he too could use it as some kind of magic symbol of power and protection.

He waited till dead of the night. A thick opaque mist hovered over the lake waters. He knew which window he could force open to enter the house. Would they be asleep? The old master's bedroom was at the other end of the house. He paused in the center of the hallway listening. Not a sound. He parted the heavy curtain to the bedroom of the sisters. A night lamp burned on the marble-topped washstand. The massive almirah stood in a corner. So many drawers. So many clothes. Blurry mirrors. His face hidden. Rummaged in the drawers. Tortoiseshell, ebony and ivory jewel boxes. Opened them. Heavy gold necklaces. Brooches. Rings. Bracelets. Crisp bank notes. Fragrances. Odors. Orris root. Lavender sachets. Camphor. A gecko-cry sounded as sharp as the notes of the striking grandfather clock. Harriet woke up. Called out to Caroline. At that moment he felt the fear of discovery. If he were caught? The prison built by the British at Bogambara. Years in a cell. Never to come out. Hanging. Death. Forgotten.

He would have to wrench open the doors but what if they woke up. He must be sure that there would be no betrayal. His hands felt that he was grasping a stalk of a plant. For a moment he was in the garden. He felt a tender stalk twisting in his hands. Grow limp. A sigh. Breath ceased. He jumped out of the window. Ran. Ran. Along winding paths overhung by ancient trees. Into the heart of the sanctuary. No one was ever to see him again.

EARLY FICTIONS: MYTH AND REALITY

I once found pages of the story I had begun to write about that house of the two sisters. They were the beginnings of that memory that was to haunt me all these years....

The old house stood by the side of the lake looking out on the vaporous mists that wreathed it, rising from the green waters that reflected, musingly it seemed, the surrounding hills, forests, sanctuaries, parks and shady trees over-hanging it. Its yellowing walls, pillared portico, wide verandah, glass paned windows were old fashioned, belonged to another age. It stood in its own garden of poinsettia and bougainvillaea and within this house lived the three members of the family, all unmarried, looked after by a band of faithful retainers, family servants.

The house was full of whispers: they seemed to emerge from every nook and cranny of it. Dust lingered on the heavy old furniture, those great Dutch antiques of calamander, ebony and satinwood, the dull brass trays, the carved walnut, the inlay work, the china wallplates, the heavy landscapes possessed of an ornateness, a dark splendor which imprisoned those frail souls. Comfort seemed to lounge, to grow plump and fat among the old furniture. The cat purred endlessly on the worn carpet while the geckoes crept along the high walls, waiting immobile, pausing, transforming the wall into a frieze of hieroglyphics – a language of silence communicable by feel, by scent, by instinct; but lost to the unseeing eyes below. On those high smooth whitewashed walls a nightly enactment of death. A mad whirl of diaphanous wings hurling themselves round the glowing fruit like globes of light in an incomprehensible passion for the searing moment, or they cast off their wings and become earth bound, their helpless carcasses pallid and oozing, carried out by the well-organised phalanxes of ants.

The sisters were as frail as two sparrows; they were an inbred family. Their bones so fine – like ivory toys. They possessed the ivory immobility of living in the ivory tower. There was no one to animate those marionette limbs, to evoke either pity or laughter. They seemed rather to be doomed to a mockery of silence, as if they had ceased to live, physically. Ceased to hear those living voices that came across the lake for they were always listening intently to those whispers that abounded in this old, dark house. The purr of the cat, the swish and scrape of brooms, the clink and clatter of domestic cutlery, the muted voices of the ageing servants seemed to carry with them echoes that were perpetually reverberating through the house. How soft and fine the parchment of their skins, the spidery patterns of their silk dresses of grey and blue, their soft strands of grey brown hair brushed smoothly over the little sparrow skulls. They were brittle, brittle, brittle, old fine bones, inhumanly fragile. No one heard the cry for love, there were no children to answer a sign or whisper or promises of chocolate kisses.

Spencer, their brother also inhabited the comfortable tomb,

so tall, so thin and gaunt in cream tussore silk suits, old drooping eagle that had no prey to clutch at. Spencer was not like Harriet and Caroline. His limbs were straight. How much did he regret. They dare not question that awful love, that had made him immolate himself with them for over half a century. They had all grown so old, waiting for death, counting each chime from the pendulum of the great grandfather clock. How violently the beat swung with the pendulum, how loud, how heavily metallic, gong-like the startling giant beat during the dark hours of the night when Harriet would wake, her mouth parched, thirsty, to reach for the carafe of water with its suspended glass tumbler. To listen to the cool talking sound of the water gave her comfort. The house was too vast for them, too full of old spacious rooms, of furniture that crowded heavily, old wood that no termite ever invaded, wood that had no living feeling which had the heart torn out of it long ago, no veins where the blood grew sluggish, thick and congealed. The hours between sleeping and waking, so long. You could hear the dry rustle of beetles rasping on window ledge, of crickets insistent clicking behind the great wardrobe, a clicking so monotonous, it hurt the reluctantly listening ear, of wings brushing against the dark, searching for an outlet. The brain was disturbed by the perpetual fumblings for escape. By morning most of them had met with their death. However slight their sound, Harriet felt the intrusion, she was afraid of hurt. She thought and thought ... dreamed ... woke ... sleeping fitfully. High above the four poster beds the spiders built their webs in the high ceiling, undisturbed. The festoons of silk were dull and heavy being untouched by dew or sunlight, a secret world that ensnared a myriad moths, mantises, cicadas, scintillating fireflies whose destiny led them surely to the spiders maw. Spiders so secret watching, waiting, mating, intent on building their snares. "You must know," thought Harriet "the horror of being old, of having misshapen limbs that could grow helpless, waiting to be helped from chairs lifted out of cars, even to watch the world passing by."

That the shadows were waiting to consume the little human

shapes of Harriet, of Caroline, of Spencer and even the cat that did nothing but dream. What else could they do in that house by the lake?

That was the house as I had once imagined it. I had thought all houses safe in my childhood. That doors could be locked against intruders, against those who would do you harm. I had learned to trust too early in life. It would take me years to know that the enemy lay close at hand. Harriet and Caroline believed that no one would want to hurt them and they had dwelt in that belief for so many years. And yet the weak and the helpless were the victims of forces that were greater than their own lives which each thought predictable. Until that destined end.

I grew up and went away to inhabit another house. Walks round the lake were few and far between. One day I was shocked at the news of the murder of one of the Bevan sisters. The gardener was the suspect my mother told me.

The gardener? Who was that unknown person? Was he the shadowy form I saw in my early dreams. I had followed him through the hallway but when he entered the bedroom, the door closed behind him. That door closed finally on my childhood too.

To whom do all these memories matter now? It all happened so long ago. Names are forgotten. Engraved only on ruined tombstones. No one remembers. They remain only in my memories, fragmented now, of that landscape which was part of my history too. The horror of that death still remains with me. I think now that the sisters could not have felt great pain. Age and feebleness are sometimes opiates. I think back now on that gardener. His life. His sense of desperation. He who gave life to seeds, bulbs, plants, why did he take that human life? I still try to answer that question although the protagonists are all dead. I enter into that vast and echoing silence of a deserted, ravaged, landscape. The cocoon of my childhood was slit violently with my newly acquired knowledge of violence – violation and history. Rebellion and its aftermath which would endure through the centuries.

Nothing can be more picturesque than the situation of

Kandy, the banks of a miniature lake, overhung on all sides by hills which command charming views of the city with temples and monuments below. In the lake, a tiny island is covered by a picturesque building, now a powder magazine but in former times a harem of the King. A road which bears the name of "Lady Horton's Walk" winds round one of those hills; and on the eastern side, which is steep and almost precipitous. It looks down on the valley of Doombera, through which the Mahaweliganga rolls over a channel of rocks, presenting a scene which nothing in the tropics can exceed in majestic beauty.

In the park at the fact of this acclivity is the pavilion of the governor, one of the most agreeable edifices in India not less for the beauty of its architecture than for its judicious adaptation to the climate. The walls and columns are covered with chunam prepared from calcined shells, which in whiteness and polish, rivals the purity of marble. The high ground immediately behind is included in the demesne, and so successfully have the elegancies of nature, that daring my last residence at Kandy a leopard from the forest above came nightly to drink at the fountain in the parterre.

– *Ceylon (Vol. II)*,
Sir James Emerson Tennent

THE SACK

The forest encircled the hamlet – so remote, so isolate. A land forgotten by all people. Border villages, they call them. The trees, standing close-knit, the branches braided together, interlocked arms encircling us. We grew with the seasons and fed on the harvests we gathered. Day in and day out we toiled on the land. We had our homes, our fields, our chenas. We had all that was sufficient for our needs. The gourds were plump in the chenas. The melons ripened in the sun, their flesh succulent, rich. The maize stalks hung weighted with yellowing grains. The pale kernels tender, a light gold, were embedded in the cobs. Water brimmed over in our wells. Milk flowed plenteously from our cattle. We set the curds in clay pots. Paddy harvested from the fields was spread out to dry on mats.

There is no one to answer the questions we ask. We cannot find the answers even within ourselves. Our minds are all wounded. Slashed with knives. Chopped with hatchets. Axe blades. Knife blades. Steel blades are silent. Blood flows out silently. Our screams sound like those of startled birds or the screeching wails of animals that emerge from the forest. The predator and its prey. It is the accepted law of the jungle. Who is there to hear our human death cries in the darkness as we are startled out of sleep?

After the massacre our village is like some old temple painting of apaya, of hell. The world from which we try to escape, by accruing merit in this life. Who knew that night would bring this world of hell to our thresholds? The shadows, so grotesque, reaching out to strangle us. My eyes, filled with the smoke of sleep, seeing the lampwick flicker on those bodies that netted us in chords, tightening, taut, so that we could not escape, caught in the bloodied web of death.

What can I do now? He lies before my eyes, my son. My hands are wet with his blood. My clothes soaked with his blood. My skin, damp with the feel of its wetness. I look at him. The gash wounds are deep. My cries are not the only cries in this desolate village. I can hear the wailing all around me. And the crackling sound of dried coconut fronds. The thatched roofs ablaze. The walls eaten up by fire. Fire tongues creeping out of long, dark, leopard shapes licking this village with an all-consuming, ravening greed.

At dawn fire-charred sticks will be left and thick mounds of ash piled up where the habitations existed. All the bundles of firewood we have gathered from the jungle of what use? Why should I ever want to place the pot of rice on the fire again? To feed whom? All the pots, washed, upturned to dry on the messa, that frame of jungle sticks, just outside the kitchen readied for the next day, shattered.

The waters of the well. Polluted. Streaked with red weals, impregnated with smells of smoke, fire, blood, death. Never to drink water from that well again. I used to bathe my son with that water when he was very young. Bucket after bucket I would draw up and pour over the naked body, the hair sleeking like wet ferns over the forehead. Black. Glistening. His clothes too I washed. Spread them out to dry in the sun.

I used to sing to him those lullabies that my own mother and grandmother sang to me.

I was a good mother to him. That was natural. I suckled him long after the time was past. He clung to my breast. He was a comfort to me. He was the amulet I wore to protect me from those malign influences that were a daily threat to life in this remote village of ours.

Wails. Screeching. They have come. And gone. Their bodies too must be covered with blood. Flesh from the killings adhering to their skin. Bodies impregnated with sweat and the smell of fear and death. Perhaps their own too have died, met death in the same manner. There's no one left now in all this world who has not lost some kith and kin through the bullet or steel blade or fire.

We were preparing for the New Year. Soon I would have pounded the paddy, then the rice, sifting the flour and toasting it in the earthenware chatty on the wood fire. Mixed it with thick honey and coconut milk to fry kewun for the auspicious day.

The harvest had been a good one. The sun was hot. The grain has dried well on the mats spread out in our compounds. Mats I had woven with my own hands from the golden strips of dried reed. Baskets and vatti too. Yes, I would make kewun. Kiribath too, cutting the new rice cooked in coconut milk into diamond shapes. Not very much more. I would prepare enough for the family and for the neighbors during that time of goodwill. Yet, I had my fears.

The flies were buzzing. It was the smell of honey that brought them, I knew, but then again, their buzzing somehow sounded more sinister, more menacing. An angry whirring, stabbing the air with so much greed. I was suddenly afraid. As if messages were arriving from other villages, far away where those dreadful events had already taken place. Would they come? When? Who? The avengers? The death dealers?

Our nights were restless. Often we would escape into the jungle and remain there until daylight. In the darkness. Afraid of the rustle of every leaf and twig. Missed the mat my body was used to, its woven strands softened by my sleeping on it night after night, its stiffness giving way to my warm flesh. The feel, the presence of other bodies filled the room. The children's father slept on the only couch we had on the pilla, the small outer space leading out from the inner rooms. If I felt thirsty I would lift the coconut shell off the water pot and drink the cool water. The chk chk of the geckos sounded from the crannies of the wall. The nights were hot, sometimes. I could hear the rasping sound of a sharp cough.

He's dead too, now. My man. And the younger children. And the children of this village like the children of all the other afflicted villages. Only you lie before me. Barely alive.

Shadows on the walls. Magnified. Grotesque. Creeping up. Stretching long. Wide. Crouched. And reaching inside. Who can understand this world of darkness, the world in which we find ourselves, now? The long shadows creep out of the night to grow on these walls. Forms. Shapes. Squat. Dwarfed.

Shadows widening then elongating. Stretching like lizards. Coiling like reptiles. Shadows that are flat but monstrous. They have no smell.

The smell lies only within the reality of physical bodies. There are two kinds of life here. The human. The shadow. They move together. Interweave. Merge.

The long shadows came out of the dark and crept up our walls. From these shadows the flame tongues licked our dwelling places and torched the thatch of our roofs. The reptiles that lurked in the straw burned to a cinder and hung like blackened, twisted ropes dangling from the eves.

Flesh shredding and tearing like cloth. Silence. Stealth. Dogs quickly silenced.

My children. Growing up. Helping in the fields. In the chena. Going to the village school. Walking along footpaths. Edged by the jungle. I would lie awake watching the shadows on the walls. Sometimes they appeared menacing. As if giving shape and form to my disturbing dreams. The room would be the forest. The walls not of clay bricks or mud sun-dried, but of the rough bark of trees. My feet rustled on a bed of dried leaves. Tiny insects crept between my toes, whirred in my ears. Ants of fear prickled on my skin. And then with dawn the familiar, the recognizable walls of the hut, the thatched roof with its rafters and beams of forest wood, was gradually restored. The sweat of my uneasy dreams dried on my skin as I readied the hearth to boil water for tea.

Suddenly the shadows are living shapes. They become fleshed. The darkness is tangled with their long limbs. Fear enters within our hearts, our minds, our bodies. Terror corrodes the veins. The blood is dark, rusting.

What am I to do now? What am I to do? My son, your life is ebbing out. I have to take you to the hospital but not through any known roads. Might encounter the predators again. Through the forest. Yes, that's the only way. I can't carry you.... Your body, inert, is a dead weight. Then how can I lift you from the ground? In what can I carry the weight of your body? Make a hammock of my cloth? No, that won't do. Then ...? Yes. The sack. The sacks are folded and put away. All the grain is used up, all the maize, sesame and millet from the chenas and the paddy from the fields. I'll take one of those empty sacks and gently ease your body into it. Drag the sack through the jungle. I can lift your body part of the way.

Blood harvest. I had such hopes for you my son. A clever boy. You could have gone away from here one day ... learned ... escape from the terror.

Ah! yes, that's what I will do. Use the empty sack.

Puthé? Son? No, you cannot talk. I'll first bind your wounds. Tear up one of my old cloths? The soft worn out ones. The ones that are used to swaddle babies with.

Why did they do this to us? How can they go back and sleep at night? Everybody has dreams. The torture of dreams. Those who commit these deeds are nameless. Faceless.

We are like trees in the chena that they set fire to, slash and burn. Hack and cut. The rest of the trees stand silently ranged round the bare, cleared space. Stumps of burned out trees. Like human torsos. Roots straggling everywhere. Stripped branches. Leaves piled up. And what will they plant in their place? Grain? Gourds? To feed whom? No, they will not wait long enough to plant their seed or harvest new crops. Merely move on and on to the next settlement and the next. All the faceless ones. Who says that they too have not suffered? Have their own loved ones not died too.

Attacks on village. Reprisal killings. Death is the new inhabitant that dwells in our village. Doesn't wait long. Death moves on and on. Those knives. Wiping the blades clean. To be used again. The compliant flesh yields so easily. Will they soon forget? Everyone will forget. And go on with their lives. Puthé. Son. Our journey has begun. I don't know whether you can hear but I'll talk. You're safe in the womb. The sack. I'll protect you.

Night seems endless.

Puthé, why have they done this to us? When can we reap another harvest? When? We laid out food for all the deities after we reaped the paddy. We carried out all our rituals. We did not forget even one. All the deities of this hamlet of ours were remembered. The sickle was laid against the sheaves of paddy. Is there a single ritual we left neglected?

Puthé, are you listening to me? From within the sack? From within my womb?

What did you feel when you saw those shadows on the walls? Did you know that they were death-bringing shadows? When can we come out of the forest? I am past fear and terror now. No, they will not harm us. The animals here. Why should they harm us? We aren't out for their blood.

Did I ever think that I would have to bear your wounded body, wrapped in blood, in this fashion? Ah! I wish I could keep you from more hurt but the path is rough. These stones gnash their teeth against your flesh, once throbbing with life.

When I looked into the faces of those strangers I saw masks. Humans that wear masks of terror and roam the villages, the ancient villages. Come to visit us. Set up their totems here. Behind those masks I could not see the faces of men or women. Faces of innocence. If I saw them as innocent I would have to see them as the children they once were. Like my own children.

But masks? No. Questions of humanity, of man or woman destroying their own kind, no longer comes into it. So let's leave it at that.

They came from another world. That's where they go back after the death dealing is over. Behind the masks, their skins are the color of rotting leaves. Their smell that of beasts that have traveled far and carried many burdens. Hunger. Thirst. Do we not share these feelings too?

"Son, puthé, are you thirsty? Let me wipe your forehead. Puthé.... You are safe now. In this sack. In my womb. Be patient with your pain. The pain which I share with you. Be patient. The darkness protects us!"

The darkness of the forest leads us through new dangers but

they are recognizable ones. The predator needs to live. My feet seek the stones of a cleared path, the rough pebbles and grating stones.

As I drag your body in this sack I now know your wounds bleed but there's no other way to take you away from the village, through the jungle and out again. My hands grip the bunched up edges of the sack and I draw it along.

Yes, you groan. Wait, I will pause. I will lift the sack with my arms in which your body lies, wipe your forehead with my palm, thread my fingers through your thick, damp hair. I'll push away the bigger stones with my foot. I'll try to make this agonizing journey easier.

You and I, alone in the dark. Alone. But I'll take you out of the forest – I will, I will. My arms are not weak. I've lifted many heavy burdens in my lifetime. I'll take you through, I will. I will bring you out of the darkness.

Whether your eyes will ever open to the light I am not certain but I know this is the only way out for us both. Through the forest. To seek a cleared footpath. To emerge out of the darkness.

THE LAST REFUGE

Alone, up on the bank near the water tank Theresa set up stakes along which the tendrilling bean plants would cling. There were bowers of bitter gourd and snake gourd. Bushes of green chillies sprang up from the seed that she scattered so prodigally. The earth was fertile up there. The winged bean creeper twined and twisted round the anodha tree. Digging, weeding, planting. Theresa ignored the world of domesticity below her. There she stood, an absorbed, meditative expression on her face in a green world surrounded by the fruit of her labor. She took bowls of water from the tank with frogs spawn floating in green bubbles on the surface and tadpoles swimming about in the murky depths. Sometimes a drowned kingfisher lay at the bottom of the tank fallen from the towering avocado pear tree.

Vegetables appeared in abundance springing up from the soil which no one had bothered to use before. Wild thorny plants, nidikumba and lantana had flourished there. You could feel that peace was a tangible quality that wrapped her, her rasping tongue stilled, a closed-in secret expression smoothening the lines on her haggard face. She offered no blandishments to make the plants grow spreading their tendrils and leaves in sun and rain. They say that plants flourish if you spoke or sang to them. Theresa did neither but her gnarled, work-worn hands touched the tender shoots with great sensitivity so that the stalks neither bent nor snapped in two. The earth that we thought unyielding pushed out shoots that grew straight and strong. That garden of her own creation became her territory.

My husband and I would return from work, go into the kitchen, light the fire and pour the tea rather than call her to help. She appeared to be at peace with herself. Her raving and ranting had ceased. What I did not understand then was that she was railing against life itself. I was just another stranger who could make arbitrary decisions about her life. Too many times the doors had been shut in her face. She had had to pack her bag and leave, drifting until she found a temporary refuge again.

I needed Theresa. She did not want to admit that she had need for me too. She helped me and my family to exist, to work, to carry on the household. What I gave her did not fulfil her deepest needs. She lived on the fringes of our lives, felt that she would never be drawn into that magic circle of kinship or the familiarity and intimacy of a close friendship. She had years of living behind her of which we knew nothing. All we had were a few glimpses of that past which she recounted of her wanderings and displacement. Food, shelter, money whatever I provided her with, did not fill that huge empty gap that yawned before us.

For five months I had been without a dependable and responsible household help to take charge while we were away at work and while our children were at school. Someone to open the door to the children, heat up their food and serve it out as they came in tired and hungry. Pots and pans, cups, saucers, plates lay piled up in the sink until we returned. Unwashed clothes had to be gathered up, rooms swept and tidied. The dust and litter had to be cleared and order restored before the next day began all over again.

One afternoon, at school, one of my fellow colleagues had drawn my attention to a woman who stood lonely and lost on the corridors.

"Ah, that's Theresa. I know her. She has worked for me in the past. A Roman Catholic. Very devout but you'll have to be careful of her if you engage her as a servant. She has a nasty temper. She needs a job she says. Must have quarreled with her family and been chased away. Nowhere to go. I don't need her.

I have a good servant. You can try her out but she's very dominating."

I looked at the old, bedraggled women draped in a white sari with a jacket that hung loose on her gaunt body. She seemed to be half-starved, yet when she spoke her voice was strong. We looked at each other through the wide stretch of years that separated us. Her knowledge of the world must be much greater than mine, wandering, lost through a vast and lonely desert, stopping briefly at the oases of strangers' homes. Neither of us had alternatives. We would have to accept each other. Where would she search for another place to stay? To be on the road at this stage of her life must have shown a desperate need.

"How much do you expect as salary?" I asked her.

"You name the amount," she said indifferently as if that were not the most important issue at stake. I was teaching in a Roman Catholic College and she probably felt confident that I would be able to understand her better. This I was to learn later. We took each other on trust but I was not sufficiently worldly wise to know that a reciprocatory relationship would not be easy. She clutched at me as a drowning man would at a straw. Sink or swim. "Help me get a firm footing on shore, help me find my bearings. I have to survive. Can't get onto the road again." Perhaps those were her unspoken thoughts. Nothing was predictable. I had been warned that she had a difficult personality. I was used to conflict but tried to make life easier for myself by resolving it or I would be the sufferer. I could not face the coldness of being rebuffed. Transformations. All the fanciful tales I had heard in my childhood spoke of good and evil personified by human beings. Our essential natures with all their flaws were carefully concealed or society would shun us.

We rationalized, negotiated, coaxed and cajoled. Theresa would be more truthful but it had not made life easier for her nor would it be easy for her in her unpredictable future. I had a purpose in mind. Survival. Like Theresa herself. Sometimes I felt I was clutching one of those old cast iron smoothing irons filled with the burning embers of coconut shells. I had to get the creases out of the garment to make myself presentable to society. The everyday attire that helped me preserve the predictable image. The social image. Sometimes my hand that held the wooden handle of the iron would slip and the searing heat singe my skin but I carried on without regard to the stinging welt. Both of us would try to live with each other. I was younger and more resilient so it would be easier for me. My husband was impervious to servants' moods. My children would learn to skirt the difficult moments in any relationship. It was I myself who would have to confront whatever lay before us.

"Wait till school is over, Theresa. You can go back home with us," I said. And Theresa entered our lives to teach me lessons I was not yet ready to learn, of loneliness, of the fears of being stranded at the crossroads of life, of age, of uncertainty, of being thrown out and betrayed by your own kith and kin. I would learn although it would take me years and years to do so. Those were rehearsals of loss and pain. The roseate hues of an illusory landscape would change, the horizon become dark and pathless.

Theresa's manner was often grim. Occasionally in her mellower moments she spoke of the house she had worked in where she had been happy. A household that broke up after the death of the old mistress and the dispersal of the family.

One day she brought out a bulging envelope from among her clothes folded and packed carefully away in a suitcase. It was full of color photographs of her previous employers, an affluent family she had worked for in Colombo. She had looked after two children. She had loved their lavish and extravagant lifestyle. Theresa had been able to boss them all. They accepted the dominance she wielded over the household. It had been a conservative Tamil family and the matriarch of the household carried out the traditional duties, the first to get up in the morning. "Very early," Theresa told us. "She would wake up before anyone of us had risen. She would prepare a big jugful of coffee for the whole household. I would not be allowed to go into the kitchen. My duty was to look after the children."

"Wasn't it difficult to look after two young children, Theresa?" I asked.

"Well, nona, I used to frighten them. Tell them frightening stories. They were afraid of me," she said grimly. "How else could I make them do as I wanted. They wouldn't have obeyed me and I would have had to run after them all the time. I made them play quiet games. One word, one look from me would quell them."

In the evenings Theresa would recite her rosary, the prayer beads draped about her fingers intoning the Hail Mary's in loud, sonorous tones. Prayer after prayer, her work-worn fingers stroking the beads as she knelt on the cold cement floor, her head bowed in suppliant pose. She chose her own penance and pleaded day in day out for the expiation of her sins. That prayer life had nothing to do with the way she lived with others. Now old, but not spent, she was working out her own salvation, uttering the prayers and litanies she had learned from those early days of her first Communion. She had never forsaken her faith and belief but had bowed her head and knelt in prayer in church after church and in the homes of strangers. She had confessed her sins, accepted the blessings of the Host. It was only when she folded her hands in prayer that she knew true peace. Years of scrubbing pots and pans, the vegetable stains, part of the texture of her skin, the nails worn down to the quick. Sculptured prayer hands. Even, as she uttered her prayers, the voice was strong, she commanded. She coerced God and Mother Mary to take notice of this penitent. She was no humble supplicant. No one could disregard those compelling tones.

It was that same voice of command she used with humans. A series of orders.

"Here." That was her mode of address to anyone of us. "Close that tap."

"Bring me betel, now don't forget, the tender leaves with

plenty of lime, tobacco and arecanut," she ordered the master of the house on his shopping expeditions.

"Close that window."

Peremptory tones. Imperatives. No polite requests. This was her way of bonding herself with us. We were part of her family. Her people spoke to her in that manner. She spoke to them too in the same way. Life was a giving of orders. A carrying out of orders. Did she see other faces when she looked at us? Perhaps she did not even notice our faces, our expressions of pain or hurt as she hurled her words at us. Who, in all her life had spoken with softness and kindness to Theresa who had no home of her own. She could not understand our love for our dogs. There was no reason why she should. In her life, dogs were an afterthought. No one had shown her kindness. That humans should use blandishments on dogs was inexplicable to her. Moreover, she had to lay claim to some little bit of territory in this house which was crowded with our lives, their happenings, the activities, the adventures, the relationships. She did not want to be pushed into the background. We never shouted at her. We never raised our voices against her. We acknowledged her importance in our lives but that was not enough, would never be enough for someone like Theresa who had been hounded out of her children's lives, considered an extra mouth to feed, a penniless woman, with no resources of her own to sustain her. Looking for a corner in a stranger's home to lay down her mat. She had to feel the strength of her voice. That life giving force that would get her attention.

"Out, out," she screamed at the dogs, "get out of my kitchen, you," she lunged at the dogs with her broom. Her territory. Closed to humans and animals. Her little space. Her kitchen. In the home she no longer had. Perhaps that's how she had been treated by her son, or her daughter. "Chased me out with a broomstick, that's what they did. Was anyone kind to me, even my own children? Look at me. They don't want me. Grudge me a little food and drink and space to sleep in. I slaved for them. I slaved for everyone. For my man too and in the end, what did I get?"

A sense of pity grew within me. I wanted to make life happier for her. I looked for ways and means to do so. Sometimes I succeeded. At others, I failed.

The dogs slunk about with their tails between their legs and cringed at the sound of her voice. They began to develop peculiar habits too. Browny would secretly jump onto the hearth and steal the food out of the pots. One day the whole fish curry disappeared. Browny's personality changed. Became subversive. Invaded Theresa's domain, ate what was denied him when his food was served by her. Theresa had a soft corner for Saucy who was given preferential treatment.

"Come Saucy, come. Your food is ready" she called out, her voice lowered. Then she would raise her voice and say, "Browny, here, eat. Greedy dog." Browny hid under the table and refused to come out. Even the children were now wary of her. She had her way of ignoring them. Turning a deaf ear if they asked for anything. Coldly, calmly carried on with a pretence of work. She was building a wall around her, a solid wall. No chinks appeared. She had been bruised and battered by her own children. She could no longer believe in anyone. "Leave me alone," her manner indicated. "Leave me in peace. It's too late for anyone to make amends. I've lost everything. Can you see what I'm reduced to? I, who had once been mistress of my own household, am now a servant. You and all the others I have worked for have no other name for me. We will always live in separate worlds. Don't try to change me. My heart is now hard. I'm set in my ways. I cannot relearn a new language in which to make life easier for myself. You are teachers. Don't try to change my mode of speech. This is the only way I can survive. By retaining this little bit of independence of my spirit or else I'll be a bent and broken branch. I'll snap apart. And who will care?"

It hurt me when Theresa sulked. Or was in a bad mood. Yet wasn't she an old woman who should have had more comforts, who if she did not feel like cooking or washing could be out in the garden tending the vegetable plants she loved. Or go to church as often as she liked, spending hours praying for solace.

Or to sit and gossip with her cronies and have her daughter bring her a cup of tea. Or a granddaughter to comb her hair or massage her body to ease it of its weariness. There was nothing like this for her.

Wasn't I always the pampered one? Did I think it would be so easy to share the home of strangers, cooking food, doing things the way others wanted? The lives of these women were so circumscribed. Cooking, grinding, pounding, washing, sometimes bone weary, exhausted with a myriad aches and pains.

Theresa tried to fit into the expected mold when she first came to us. We were working folk with young school going children. We took our lunches with us as we had a long day at school. Theresa used to get up early, to prepare our lunches during those first days, but soon she began to change things to suit her. She stored food in the refrigerator to be heated up the next day. The food was unappetizing, everything tasted the same. Sometimes it was even stale. Like a child she began to prepare little delicacies for herself. She had the freedom to do whatever she liked. When I went into the kitchen to prepare a special dish I would be amused to find small bowls of blancmange, toasties, fried eggs, and hot cups of coffee. "Ah, at last you feel at home," I thought to myself and yet why didn't Theresa think we would like her to prepare special things for us too? I couldn't question her. I didn't dare to. This was her private space and she could give herself the little pleasures that gave her a bit of happiness.

Theresa must have felt the rigors of age. Although she looked strong, her hair thick black with hardly a strand of grey in it as a result of all the coconut oil she applied on it daily, her body was tired. Tired. She found it difficult to wake early as we did and to conceal her unease to find us up and about. She would stalk loftily into the kitchen and ignore our presence. Lift the lid of the pan in which water was boiling for the coffee and bear it off to wash her face. After she had finished her ablutions she would stalk in again and pour herself a cup of coffee. She had, I think, got tired of us all. Tired of being a servant. Tired of the only role in life she had been forced to follow to keep body and soul alive. She just gave in, grew indifferent to our needs. Became slipshod and careless as if her arms could barely lift the dishes and plates to the sink to be scrubbed.

The cooking utensils were greasy, with smudges of soot marks, dirty spoons were merely wiped and put away on the plate rack. Sometimes she carried on a monologue, complaining about her lot in life. Sometimes her face lengthened as she sulked. She was lonely. No one to talk to. No one to gossip with over the fence. Nor did she want to visit her relatives. She wanted us all to stay in the house, not to go out and leave her alone. She began to resent our friends visiting us. When they came, she would go into her room and lock herself in, shutting out the sounds of conversation and laughter. If the visitors stayed till too late she would go about banging doors and shutting windows.

When old servants came visiting and I asked her to give them food or tea, she would grow angry. "What, make tea and give her? Look at the price of milk and sugar. Hmm, tea then lunch and after that … is she going to spend the night here? Is she going to spend a few days? Where's the room for her? Don't ask me to share my room with her, she's sure to keep me awake," she said in a grumbling voice.

For herself, Theresa would hide bottles of sugar, rice, tea, coffee as if suddenly she would find there was nothing left for her. She would cook special dishes for herself and then give up halfway. Hide it all away, forget where the hiding place was. The food spoiled, fungi would sprout, mold cover it with a grey-blue film, strange smells emanate from corners behind the cooker and everything would have to be thrown away. Yet she was an excellent cook. She sliced, grated, stewed, stirred. She broiled, tempered, simmered. Her soups were thick, redolent of onions and karapincha-leaf tempered in coconut oil, potatoes, dhal, everything went into the pot. Carrots, cabbages, celery. Crisp croutons floating on top. Her soups were like magic potions. Gave life and energy. Her imagination rioted in their preparation. She delighted in setting the pot on the roaring flames of the woodfire burning on the earth. Her own nature was closer to that simmering pot seething within a flurry of cooking vegetables in its own turmoil of bubbles and flavors. A soup full of surprises.

Theresa was never meant for one of those small kitchens in little houses. She needed a smoke-filled kitchen with blackened walls and huge clay pots with a hiramane to scrape coconut and a grinding stone for spices. She needed stacks of firewood and coconut husk to light the fires, pyramids of coconuts piled in a corner of the kitchen, an atuwa with paddy, pettagams filled with rice. Jars of condiments. She wanted a large jar from which she could ladle salted fish. She had all this in the household of the wealthy Tamil family she had worked for. She needed to talk in loud tones and bully and scold and shout and go to mass, to say her prayers out aloud and feel victimized and persecuted and collect wads of money and eat secretly the little delicacies she shared with no one. Our family was all wrong for her. We didn't provide her with the excitement she needed to sustain life, to relieve her of the burden of boredom and loneliness.

Theresa hated to be excluded from the parties and dinners we had. I sometimes had to summon the courage to go into the kitchen, to step over that invisible boundary she had set up, to tell her, "Theresa, tonight we will have guests for dinner."

"Hmm" she muttered under her breath.

"I have decided to serve stringhoppers, fish curry, cutlets, seeni sambol … I'll make the caramel custard."

Sometimes Theresa would not even respond with a nod. Cold silence greeted me. She would get into one of her moods so that none of us could approach her. In dead silence she would begin to prepare the food and glare ferociously at anyone who would come into the kitchen.

"Theresa," I would try to explain apologetically. "We can't always eat off other people in their homes. We must repay the hospitality of our friends. Surely you would do the same thing in your home?"

"And when did I have my own home. That was a long time ago when my man was alive. Now I can't even live with my own daughter. She is always quarreling with me. She doesn't want me in her home. I'm a burden to her. Go away, go away she says. That's why I am here. If I leave you I have to search for another place. What a pity that old household broke up after the old mistress's death. Oh, the pans of hot hoppers. The coffee she made. And all I did was to look after the children."

"Theresa, please prepare the food well tonight. You are so much more experienced in cooking than myself. It is true I have my own home with my family around me, a loving family but think, how many hours can I spend here? Working from morning to night, I can't give up. I have children to bring up, to feed, clothe, educate."

"Hmm," was all she said. She dropped the knife. It fell on the floor with a clatter.

It just missed my foot. I stepped aside instinctively.

"Theresa," I exclaimed, anxiously. "What did you drop? What fell from your hand?"

"Whatever it was that fell," she answered tersely.

The kitchen knife lay at my feet, the cutting edge towards me. I picked it up, washed the knife blade and put it aside. She had no intention of doing so.

I took the pudding bowl in my hands.

"Are you going to put that on the fire?" she indicated the bowl that I was going to put into the steamer.

"Yes," I said, "It will take time to be steamed. It has to be chilled too for the dessert."

I was not ready to battle with her, to spoil the evening we had looked forward to so much. Entertaining friends, planning the menu, enjoying conversation and the pleasure in the meals we prepared, gave us happiness too. Sometimes I prepared surprise dishes, whole steamed fish, roast stuffed chicken, yellow rice and rissoles, scooped pineapples and water melons filled with fruit salad. All for our friends. Theresa felt left out. Her territory and peace of mind disturbed. And when would she have time for her evening prayers?

Theresa must have waged daily battles in her daughter's kitchen, fighting for space to breathe, knowing that she was not wanted there. Whose face did she see when she looked at me, spoke to me? All faces were the same to her. Strangers. Not friends. Waiting to find fault with her, pull her up, say that her work was not satisfactory.

Christmas came and Theresa watched the preparations being made in our household. She was curious about all the gifts that were being brought home, toys, clothes, books ... she wanted to know to whom each gift was going to be given.

I had brought her a finely patterned white voile for a jacket and a flowered cloth. Theresa sewed her own jackets trimmed with handmade lace, large, loose white jackets with innumerable safety pins of all sizes fastening the front opening.

During the season and on Christmas day her nature had softened somewhat. On Christmas eve she spoke throughout of going to midnight mass but it rained heavily until past midnight and so Theresa decided to say her prayers in her bedroom. On Christmas day she prepared a wonderful lunch of chicken curry, potatoes, brinjal and stuffed capsicum, she drank arrack, ate Christmas cake and did not display her usual choleric temperament. New Year's day dawned and waking up early in the morning she roused us all greeting us in loud accents. "Happy New Year my mistress. Happy New Year my master and you children."

Would it last, this happiness of hers? Was she prepared to turn over a new leaf. I knew in my heart of hearts that the happiness she felt was something transient. She could not help herself. Always on the defensive. Too long to think anyone could feel kindly towards her. She didn't trust anyone. She had lost faith in life itself. Life to her was a battle. She felt she was surrounded by the enemy, had to protect the last vestiges of dignity she had left.

"Can't we have some peace Theresa?" I asked her. "Don't fight against all of us." Being a woman, being women, I wanted a different relationship, not one in which she saw me as her persecutor. Haunted by the past. I could not dispel the demons that pursued her. A troubled woman who could not articulate her misgivings, her distrust of human beings.

I lacked the understanding that would have helped her. Why this anger Theresa, this perpetual anger against all of us?

"Why do you say hurtful things to us?" I asked her once.

"Why what have I done?" She replied.

I wanted a truce that would last. To put an end to her bossing us, dominating us.

What's the story of your life, Theresa? Who has wounded you so much? I lacked the time, the energy to sit and listen to her. Her tale of woe. She couldn't forget the son-in-law and daughter who had chased her away. She had been starving when she came to my home. Gaunt. Her bones jutting out. Her jacket hanging loose on her big slightly sloping frame. Desperate. Hungry. Homeless. "Ah, you be careful of her. She's a good cook but hot tempered. Temperamental. I know her only too well." Remembered words. I depended on her too. I needed her. I was realistic enough to know that I couldn't go back to the past to my pampered childhood. Perhaps her mind was unhinged by her suffering. She saw us as a close united family and herself as a lonely, unwanted, unloved old woman. Her only son was paralyzed, living far away in Kekirawa. She spoke of him with sadness and sorrow yet she never helped him, never sent him any money. She collected wads of notes in a box kept under the bed but she never spent any of it on herself. Her soap, her betel, her clothes were all provided by me. Theresa also collected a charity allowance. She would wear a white or grey georgette sari and with her umbrella and purse set out by bus to go to the Kachcheri in Kandy. Sometimes she would bring the children a little brown paper bag of thala guli full of jaggery and sesame seed. This was a trip she never missed, counting the days on the calendar. It was an outing for her to be away from the monotony of her life.

"What do you want with all this money Theresa?" I asked her.

"My shroud and my coffin," she would say.

"Don't worry Theresa, who knows, you may outlive everyone.

There is a long time more for you." It was a real fear she had of a pauper's death.

"Theresa, this afternoon two Catholic priests are coming to tea." I thought she'd be happy. She reacted in the strangest possible way. She didn't want to have anything to do with them. She who had made those yards of exquisite beeralu lace for their vestments. Crocheted lace for altar cloths. She who had gone faithfully to mass, still made confession. She who many many years before had had her first Communion. The innate sinfulness of human nature ingrained in her. She shut herself up in the kitchen and sulked. She refused to have anything to do with the whole affair. My husband and I made the sandwiches, the cutlets, cut the cake. At the same time we ran around looking after the children, frying eggs for them and making tea. Theresa banged the plates and dishes on the table almost making them not to eat and then crept back into the kitchen, its warmth and comfort where she sat and ate bread, butter and jam.

One day Theresa fell ill....

"Theresa, you must see a doctor," we entreated her.

"No, no, if I go to hospital I'll die. It will be the end for me."

She lay in bed and mourned and groaned all night while we did our best to minister to her.

One morning she woke up and announced.

"I will go home."

Where was home to her? With her son or with her daughter and son-in-law? She did not give us an address. We put her in the car and dropped her at the bus stand with her bulging suitcase filled with new clothes and money.

How silent the house was after she had left. We missed the sound of her voice as she intoned the Hail Mary's on her rosary. We did not hear from her for a long, long time and so we had to find another servant to take her place.

Theresa returned unexpectedly.

"I am now well. I have come back to work." Then she still had some feeling for us. At least she had not abandoned us.

She felt what I had always wanted her to feel, that she had a safe place to stay for as long as she wanted. I was sad to tell her that we now had a new servant. Where would she go?

"I will go to a convent. I'll find a place there to end my days," she told me.

That then would be the best refuge where she would rise at dawn to recite her prayers, carry her rosary everywhere she went and have peace, dreaming of those yards and yards of lace she had made for the altar cloths and vestments, filled with the familiar symbols of her faith, the angels, the cherubs, the heavenly lilies and the crosses, hundreds of them perhaps. The crosses that she herself had had to bear through life. The crosses which I was left to carry in my own life too, many years later.

THE ADOPTION

She bent her head over the desk and wiped away the trickle of tears that welled up in her eyes.

"Madam, I do not tell anyone about my sorrows," she said haltingly. "It is only when I am with my friends that I can find happiness. When I share in their laughter, then I feel lighthearted. I can forget everything that causes me those sleepless nights."

Sharmini was one of my students and would follow my lectures on poetry and fiction as if what I spoke of, often bore relevance to her own experience of life. I too, perhaps resembled her in that manner when I was young. I felt close to this young girl who somehow seemed apart from the other students in her individualistic manner of dressing, in her soft voice, her dreamy smile. The students would often talk about their hopes and ambitions, their homes, their parents, brothers and sisters. Sometimes, they would be away for weeks and to my question, "Where have you been …?" The answer was often, "My sister or my brother was getting married. I was the bridesmaid. We had so much to do at home, preparing for the wedding."

Sharmini would remain silent while the others would talk of the difficulty of getting buses to travel to lectures, setting out early, reaching home late unless they found boarding places, going home for weekends.

"Sharmini, with whom do you live?" I once asked as the students chattered about their lives in villages outside the township of Kandy.

"With my grandparents," she whispered softly.

"Don't you ever go to your parents' home during the holidays?"

"No, never. I am always with my grandmother. I was brought up by her."

"Don't you miss your parents?"

"They come to see me sometimes. But I don't go home anymore."

Sharmini usually sat in the front row of the class. A faint, enigmatic smile often hovered about her lips. Her eyes, amber colored, lent an inward look to her expression. She appeared to be lost in a world of her own. I was not aware that she wore a mask to hide her feelings. Sharmini was a tall, slender girl. Her complexion was a light gold in colour. Her amber eyes were like transparent pools of light on which the sun shimmered. Her hair stylishly curled, rested in a wave brushed off her wide forehead. She always wore dazzling hair clips like dragonflies entwined in her hair and loops of colored ribbons tying back the strands. Beads round her neck. Bracelets and bangles on her slender wrists. The design and cut of her clothes were unvarying in style. A skirt, a blouse with elbow length sleeves. A collared jacket. Modest but elegant. A tiny cross of gold hung from the chain that encircled her throat. Her smile was enchanting. It attracted many of the young male students to her. They would stand on the corridors, somewhat apart from each other, a space, a distance between them. A delicate barrier which indicated that she would not encourage too close an intimacy.

Sometimes her face took on an expression of sadness when I spoke of family relationships in the poems and short stories we read together. Broken relationships. Family disunity. The polarization of feelings between husband and wife, mother and children. Sharmini's expression would be pensive as she listened. I sometimes felt a sense of embarrassment as if I were speaking of her own personal life.

One day she brought photographs to show me. Photographs, black and white, taken with a Kodak camera, of her mother as a young woman – sari modishly draped, bouffant hairdo.

Snapshots of her father. Her younger brother. Herself as a little girl. Her grandparents.

"Where is your home, Sharmini?" I asked her.

"My house is in Colombo madam, in a Housing Estate. It has two bedrooms. One is used by my brother. The other by my parents."

"Then where do you sleep when you go home for the holidays?"

"I can't go home now … I used to. I am happy with my grandparents. My grandparents have always cared for me. Looked after me from the time I was a child."

One day Sharmini was weeping bitterly when I went into the lecture room. She had been walking alone along a deserted playground after lectures, on her way back home. It was not a safe place to wander alone late in the evening.

The Head of the English Department had admonished her.

"Sharmini, you must be careful, young girls like you must not go by yourself when it's growing dark. We are responsible for you – you must go home straight after lectures. What were you doing on that deserted playground so late, and so far from college?" Sharmini had fixed her eyes innocently on her teacher. "Madam," she said hesitantly, "I had missed the bus."

"Be careful next time … it must not happen again. You must make it a point of going directly back home after classes."

After the lecturer had left the room, Sharmini laid her head on the desk and wept. Her handkerchief crumpled in her hand was sodden with tears. I had walked into the lecture room at that moment.

"Wipe your tears, Sharmini, you may go out and wash your eyes and then come back," I said. "You must be careful. It is not safe walking about alone these days. Especially alone."

"No Madam, I missed the bus which would take me home." She made no other explanation. She was not prepared to admit anything of her secret assignations. The lecturers were protective, concerned. Sharmini walked guilelessly against the wind. Whichever direction it blew in. She reminded me of myself when I was young. I too did not think of the dangers I might find myself in. Even as a schoolgirl I would take off on those solitary walks along lonely roads for miles and miles. No one knew where I had been until I returned home. I wanted to be alone with myself, my thoughts, going past the wild abandoned tea-estates, hills covered with trees and tall grasses, a bat-infested tunnel. A longing to be by myself would overtake me and I would open the gate and walk out. I had that freedom. But times had changed. Sharmini had walked late past the place where the toddy drinkers gathered each evening. It was not a safe road to take and the buses back home at that hour were few and far between.

One day she told me that she had gone for an interview as an air hostess.

"I don't think if I'll get the job, madam. I wish I could be more fluent in English."

"Well, I said, you have poise. You would be very good. The English you know is sufficient. And you're always so well groomed. Soft spoken too."

The months passed. Holidays. Term time. Examinations. Dissertations to be written. Sometimes my students brought kewun to class after a sister's wedding. Roshani was very attached to her elder sister and to her parents. She had been the bridesmaid for her sister's wedding and brought photographs to show us, of herself, of the bride and groom. Roshani was always going home for weekends. The students prattled innocently about their homes. Even Rohan, one of the boys, was very proud that he could cook a meal by himself. "I can even make sweets, puddings, kalu dodol, and cook rice and curry," he told us.

Sharmini was always silent. One by one, the students began to leave the English classes. They entered University or got jobs. They became teachers. Obtained scholarships to study abroad. Trained as nurses. It looked as if Sharmini would continue till the end of the course.

I was reading through a book of short stories, thinking about the one I had chosen to read with them ... when Sharmini came upto me. We were alone together.

"I want to talk to you, Madam."

"Come, sit down. What do you want to tell me?"

"Madam, I'll tell you the whole story of my life one of these days. I keep everything in my heart. I don't want anyone to know how I feel. My parents want me back now but my grandmother refuses to part with me. She won't allow them to take me back. She won't let me go."

"Whom are you more attached to, your parents or your grandmother?" I asked her.

"My grandmother. From the time I was a child she looked after me. She took the place of my mother."

"But your mother ...?"

"She was too young, too inexperienced ... just out of school. The last time they came, my parents, they cried and begged that my grandmother should allow me to go with them but she was adamant. I too cannot bear to leave my grandmother now. I am too attached to her."

"Can they not share you?"

Sharmini was silent. Then she began to speak.

"Now it has become a big fight ... this conflict between them is painful. My parents want to go to court. They have initiated a case ... to claim me ... how can they do that to my grandmother, after she has brought me up and looked after me all these years? It was not my choice. My mother made the choice voluntarily ... she ... gave me over to someone else ... she could have tried to bring me up ... I was then a burden ... I can't forget that it was my grandmother who did everything for me. Where was my mother when I cried or was hungry? I slept beside my grandmother night after night. I felt so safe, so secure, feeling her presence beside me. If only my mother had made an attempt, even struggled, to bring me up I would have had more feeling for her. Now that I am grown-up, becoming independent, now that the difficult days are over why does my mother want me? It is not that I don't understand. Perhaps, she herself is more secure, more settled. Perhaps her husband, and I do not even know whether he is my real father, is understanding. Perhaps she has carried this load of guilt in her mind all these years. She has a son now. I do not even know for certain whether he is my half brother, and perhaps she longs for a daughter. To retrieve what she has lost. Does she think it is easy to take me away from the one who mothered me all these years? What about my grandmother's feelings? My own feelings – I don't feel I want to be a kind of possession to be claimed in this manner.

"Madam, you told us the story of that Chalk Circle ... but here, it's not my true mother I want to go back with ... we hardly know each other. It would take too long, too much fresh pain, too many unanswered and unasked questions, too much tension and silence between us – and we cannot be certain of reaching a resolution. I'll even hurt her, make her feel guilty. I can't go through her suffering. We are strangers to each other now. Living with strangers, getting to know them afresh ... I don't want to be treated as a lost child. I don't want to be pampered, to feel that someone wants to make it up to me ... the weight of someone else's conscience is more than I can bear...."

"It has happened before, Sharmini," I said. "People feel a sense of desperation, unable to cope. Your mother was young. She wanted to get on with her life, she was terrified of the consequences of carrying the burden all by herself. She felt the best years of her life were still to be lived. When you're young you think sometimes of how to clear your pathway, remove impediments, obstacles on your passage. She might have thought the separation was only temporary, that one day you would return to her ... she wanted you ... she placed you in safe hands too ... she feels confident now that she can have you back in her life, offer you a home ... and your grandmother with the wisdom of age, can she not try to understand ... to share you ... but Sharmini, what do you yourself really want?"

"I am not even sure that my mother will be kind to me ... suppose we don't get on ... suppose she expresses a sense of regret, reproves me ... there will be problems. I know there will be. I am used to my grandmother's home – the house is spacious, there is a large garden. I have my own friends. There isn't even enough room in my mother's house. And won't my brother resent me? Coming into his life at this stage, displacing him. My life is peaceful now. There is no conflict … I don't have to face my mother's unhappiness … I know she's there. I accept her as my mother and yet there is so close a bond now between my grandmother and myself that I cannot think of breaking it. She has no one else but me and I think, now that she's growing old that I should not leave her. All these years, everything was provided for by my grandparents – my clothes, my education, my pocket money, books, trinkets, jewelry and so much of love and security…."

How could I arbitrate? What could I tell her? Her mother could never hope to recapture that lost childhood of her daughter. On either side of the Chalk Circle stood the grandmother and the mother. Neither wanted to relinquish her. It would only be for a brief space of time that she would remain with either of them, whatever choice was made for her. The time would come when she would walk away, free from both of them. She was worn out by their squabbling over her. Her eyes searched for a way out through the labyrinth of other people's emotions.

"Madam, she said and smiled at me. I can step over that Circle, can't I? – nothing can compel me to follow either one or the other. I'll find my own way. But till then there is room enough in my grandmother's house. I am not kept under lock and key there. When the time comes I'll move away from all these ideas of possession, of belonging to anyone. I won't give up my freedom so easily … nor will I fall into the same snare that my mother did. No, it is now time for me to step outside of that Circle. To make my own journeys, yes, to make my own choices. One day that Circle will be empty. None of us will remain. The Circle itself will be effaced."

THE CRY OF THE KITE

The sea is a brilliant turquoise under the sun; leaping on its waves silver glints of light flash like the myriad fish escaping from flung nets of sun-shadow. The whole landscape is filled with waves of white hot heat that stuns the senses and strikes the white porous sculptures of limestone at whose heart light enters carrying a whiteness that is pure silver. The sea turns silver, the blue concealed, the spray enters the atmosphere and becomes one with the shimmering particles of light. Dark green cacti grow out of the red soil, stunted bushes, sparsely scattered, ash grey branches spiked with sharp thorns interlocked entwine closely together, some of them laden with small hard-skinned custard apples. Wild flowers of brilliant color, red, purple, yellow, spring out of the red earth.

The land is so flat, so level that perspectives however distant, reach the eye without stress. The palmyrah groves merge with the shore, the shore gently touches the verge of the sea and beyond the horizon the sea and sky are almost indistinguishable. The talonic palmyrah fronds are starkly blue-black, through their serrated rows, the sea glitters silver. The wind rustles through them, swishing, swishing, with the sound of breaking waves. Black and white goats wander about in search of plants growing among the scattered limestone, those sun-sculptures created out of white sands, white spray, white shells, white light. The traveling eye rests on the ruined gopuram of an ancient temple now abandoned and exposed to the elements. The stone lingam and yoni still remain untouched by the ravages of time. The past merges into the landscape. It is a sacred land instinct with the presence of the gods and goddesses worshipped for generations, century after century.

From the garden comes the creak of the well-sweep as the old man Appu walks up and down its length tilting the bucket into the deep well. It fills with clear mineral tasting water which tilts, sparkling into a stone trough and flows gushing into earth drains which the old man's wife, Kandathe digs, to irrigate the young mango, coconut and pomegranate plants.

The wild pigeons perch on the lintel of the door; green parrots fly across the garden. On the road, thavil sound with a hard staccato beat. The brittle stillness crumbles like porous limestone into sharp splintery white dust. A funeral procession passes the house on its way to the shore where the cremation takes place, the smoke rising into the palmyrah palms from the funeral pyres, the ashes placed in their burial urns and flung into the sea after the rituals of death have been performed. Close to the margin of the shore the burial urns lie scattered and broken in the shallow water, first borne on the wave and brought back as the waves ebb and flow in their endless rhythm; they lie cracked and empty tangling with green seaweed. Little fish swim in and out of the hollow urns, the ashes mingling with sea wave, flow out into the green ocean. White seabirds swoop over the glittering fish.

We had come to Keerimalai to spend a holiday by the sea, Arasan, myself, Parvathi and Dewasundari. Arasan's birthplace was Navaly, some miles away in the interior, in the house of his forefathers, buried deep within the darkness of palmyrah groves. Here, he had spent his childhood wandering among the desolate acres of sand and rocky limestone, a landscape creating its own timelessness with its ancient fruit trees, brilliantly plumaged birds, lonely temples inhabited by gods whom he would often encounter. The supernatural was part of his habitat and part of his life. The munis dwelt in the tamarind and banyan trees. Kali and Amman temples stood among the sand dunes. The fattened goats were sacrificed in the velvi ritual, their blood splashing on the stone from the severed necks.

Walking through the paddyfields and sand dunes he would come to the little groves enclosed in silence where the temple of Amman stood. There was an ancient swing there, made by children ages ago for their play and on this swing Amman, it was said, would gently swing to and fro, in the wind. Arasan would see through his innocence, Bhairava, in the quivering trident and Amman who appeared to him out of the stillness of the groves among the tall sentinel avenues of palmyrahs, the apparition of his dreams as he wandered about alone among the green parrots and wild guavas. She appeared to him behind the thickly growing trees, stepping out of shadow and vanishing, while the grove settled back into its habitual silence and aloneness.

It has been many years since he had left Navaly, perhaps over fifteen years. Arasan was reluctant to go back.

"If I go back, will there be anyone left even to recognize me – will there be anyone alive even to remember. I too have grown away from that life."

Looking through the glass windows of the house in Keerimalai he spoke as if he beheld several visions of the past simultaneously.

"Yes, we lived there, sometime alone, my brothers and I, through the different seasons. You should have seen the serpents and scorpions during the rainy season. Blue black scorpions, glittering snakes and in our ears the eternal croak of frogs from the kerny, the temple water tank, all through the dark nights, with the sound of rain falling. Yet we were never afraid – the gods of the grove were so familiar to us, my mother would often hear the chuckle of Murugan during those long, lonely evenings. Yes, perhaps we should go. You children will never experience that life. Nothing will ever be as it once was. Years have passed since I even came this way. Aachchi and Pata are too old to come now even for the temple ceremonies. Only the caretakers, a Brahmin couple, look after the place now. We had a pond there, I remember, with lotus. There were pomegranate trees in the ul-muttham, flowers too," he mused.

"How often I used to lie on a mat under the mango tree on

those hot afternoons, the blossoms falling on my body and my mother reading out aloud from the Ramayana or the Mahabharata. We used to walk miles through the paddy fields and dunes to go to the temple festivals in the next village, carrying lanterns across those lonely spaces.

"Anyway Ponnambalam mama and Sellathe will still be there. Children, you can see the temple where your grandfather used to take part in the Kodiyetham ceremony. He gave his land to build the veedhi of the Ganesh temple. It was there that the priest once created his Pancha Muga Vinayagar and the four of us sang Sanskrit slokas in the midst of that vast crowd as the god was being taken in the chariot.

"Perhaps Kandian and Sinnian will be there too. Oh, they were so good to us when we were children. They picked fruit for us whenever we wanted, mangoes, nungoo, guavas, ichampalam. Sinnian caught wild parrots for us and squirrels....

"We used to make those huge kites too – they were so big, really enormous. We tied them to the trees and all night we could hear that deep, deep hum through its reed throat. As the wind rose and the kite soared higher and higher, the night was filled with its crying sound – the vinkoovel – how huge those pattams were, Kandian and Sinnian had to strain their muscles to hold them down as they tied them to the trees.

"I really ran wild in Navaly, playing among the desolate sand dunes with Sita and Devi, picking guavas, bathing in the kerny by the old abandoned Kalavadai Amman Kovil.

"The temples there are really ancient older than time. Their stones glowed like red jewels in the sun."

But then Arasan's life had changed. The glass windows suddenly blurred, the haze of heat swam in waves shimmering against the panes, the spray rose from the waves obscuring the horizon. From behind Sunderam's house, smoke from a funeral pyre rose in the air.

The journey began in the morning before the sun was up. We drove along miles of straight roads with groves of palmyrah palms on either side. In gardens enclosed by woven fences, were trees laden with heavy green bunches of itherai plantains. Men perched like dark birds on the well-sweep which carried up buckets of fresh mineral filled waters, falling in sparkling jets over the plants which sprouted like green feathers from the red earth. The road was empty, the houses silent behind enclosures of plaited palmyrah.

We entered the village of Navaly. The car stopped before great wrought iron gates. They were closed. Beyond them the grove of palmyrah stretched before us, the earth dark in the shade yet lit from within by traceries of sunlight filtering through blue-black fronds. A carpet of yellow margosa flowers and palmyrah fruit covered the ground. Dark avenues of straight limbed palmyrah palms led in endless rows into the unrevealed interior where the house lay, secluded and hidden.

I looked at Arasan. He stood like a stranger at his own gates, reluctant to enter. Along this road the tirrikai used to take his father away to Colombo after the weekend. Saravanamutthu Thiagarajah would wordlessly puff away at his cigar lost in his own thoughts. His son never uttered a word but sat silently beside him glad to be chosen by his father on this early morning journey to the railway station. The cart would jog along slowly on the empty road. Arasan would come back alone, alighting from the cart and go in search of Kandian or Sinnian to pluck fruits for him. The trees were laden with fruit. Birds and squirrels abounded in the grove.

Sometimes during the cholaham season the great kites would be tied by strong ropes to the trees lifted high up by the wind. All night long they would hum, the vinkoovel, a wild tearing sound like the great brass-throated nadhesweran of the temple festivals. The pattams were immense man-sized kites sometimes shaped like fish or birds. Through the dark they sang, in the wind their huge shapes floating across the face of the moon and sailing through seas of cloud. The wind tugged at them so fiercely that two or three men had to hold the thick ropes which controlled their release. In their movement upward they seemed to bear the whole grove with them, tearing up the earth, roots and all, in their upthrust.

Arasan stood uncertain on the road before the unopened gates. The road was silent and empty. Ponnambalam mama, had come in his marriage procession along this very road leading from Manipay to Navaly, garlanded and heralded by the nadhesweran and thavil, the road which for Arasan had led far and away from the village.

The carved stone elephants which had flanked the gates on the stone parapet wall had vanished.

"Why don't you open the gate?" I asked. "Why do you hesitate? It's your home."

"I'm not sure whether anyone will remember or even recognize me. I will first see whether the Nagalingams are still next door."

He walked up to the old two-storied house next to their garden. Mrs. Nagalingam had lived there for years. The children from the two houses had played together until they grew up and left the village. The wide, sloping roof, half-tiled, half-thatched was thickly covered with yellowing leaves which had fallen from the over-hanging tamarind trees. Some strangers came to the door. A woman spoke in undertones to Arasan. He walked back to where we were standing. "Mrs. Nagalingam is dead. None of her people live here any longer. The house had been rented out to a family from another village," he said.

We turned again towards the tall gates. Arasan opened them slowly. They had not been locked but were heavy and difficult to move. People seldom went in and out of them these days. We began to walk through the grove moving out of the darkness and light of shade and sunlight. In a stone trough, margosa seeds were piled closely together. The ground was thickly strewn with margosa flowers and fallen palmyrah fruits, their blue-black skins shot with a crimson sheen. The yellow flowers were bright on the alari-poo trees and their green fig-like fruits a tender yellow green, transparent lanterns through which light shone, a pale gold. Clusters of green firm-skinned mangoes hung from laden branches. No one plucked them. With the seasons, the blossoms gave way to fruit which ripened in the sun. Birds fed on them as they fell from the trees to rot, spoiled fruit, until the seed, buried in the red soil, began to germinate once more. Wild parrots swooped among the trees and behind the leaves birds sang. They flew higher and higher undisturbed with wisps of dried grass between their beaks. There were no human voices, no whispers, cries or echoes, there was a stillness in the air as of time suspended, patterns of sunlight, stretching tenuously across the grove in cobwebs of light from tree to tree. We walked, looking searchingly about us for the house, our feet sinking into piles of yellow margosa flowers, the petals, so delicate, that the morning flowers were already browning at the edges and turning the color of earth.

Arasan picked up a few petals and breathed in their aroma. They smelt of sun and earth. "Ah, we use to gather these flowers every morning," Arasan mused. "Mats were spread under the trees to collect them. They fell like rain all night and we filled baskets with them."

"And what did you do with the flowers?" Parvathi asked. "Ate them," he answered. "What a bitter, acrid flavor they had. I can still taste it on my tongue. I don't suppose Sellathe bothers to gather them anymore."

"Look, there's the house." White walls, a long empty verandah with white pillars, a closed door.

"Your old house," I said. Empty, deserted, the verandah bare, the heavy doors bolted and barred, only the footsteps of the shade crept silently nearer and nearer to its steps, the long shadows mounting upto the threshold and lying on the cold stone of the verandah.

"Is there no one here?" I asked.

"A Brahmin couple looks after the place. Let's go in search of them."

In a circle of shade two women were talking together, one of them was plump and grey-haired. The other in a dark blue cotton sari, her nose ring sparkling in the sunlight, was the Brahmin woman. The woman in the white sari turned round at the sound of our hesitant footsteps. Holy ash lay thickly on the furrows of the brow, a deep crimson tilak fell like a petal out of it. A smile of recognition wreathed her face. "Oh! Arasan thambi, is it really you? You have come back after so long. Is this your family? Come to my house, you remember it, don't you? See, it is on the other side of the road, close by, it's near the alari-poo tree. Come, come, we can drink tea. Your children, Arasan thambi, two girls! How time has passed and we have not even felt it."

While she was talking, a tall, gaunt woman flashed out of the heart of the grove. Arasan was startled. Once in his childhood Amman had appeared to him out of the stillness of an afternoon, her white sari like a wing of sunlight. Amman, the apparition of his dreams as he wandered among the wild parrots and green guavas. She had appeared, almost momentarily and then vanished, the grove settling back into its habitual stillness and silence.

"Sellathe," he cried. Her nose ring with its single sparkling diamond held his eye with its white fire. "Arasan, come with me," she said, brushing Manonmani aside. Her forehead was lined, aged, streaked with holy ash. At the parting of her still black hair a red path of kum-kumum lay, the symbol of marriage. A brilliant red tilak was stamped on her skin. "Come," she said drawing him towards her, "come, Rasa, bring your wife and children to see your mama." Her thin sinewy body, sun browned and taut was yet vigorous with life, a tightened bowstring. She enclosed us all in her possessiveness.

"Arasan, come, children come and see your mama. Where have you been all these years? Mama wrote to you when we were building our house about ten years ago, but you didn't even answer our letter. The rest of your family hardly ever comes this way now. Who will perform the Kodiyetham ceremony at Chinthamani Pillaiyar Kovil this year?"

Arasan was silent for a while, "Father is too old now," was all he could say. Sellathe continued to talk unceasingly. "Then one of you, one of his sons, must take over his duties. Have you forgotten the home of your ancestors? Who is left to maintain the respect of your family in this village? Everything has changed, mama and I are left alone at Navaly. The doors of your home are closed. Come this year at least for the festival. One of you can perform the Kodiyetham."

We were walking through the pathways between the palmyrah trees, the shadows closing round us like a net of darkness. Sellathe would not give Arasan a chance to talk. "Mama and I are now left alone to fend for ourselves. If there is no one from your family to perform the ceremonies at the temple this year, who will give us respect? Do you want your family to be forgotten? Have you forgotten your ancestors who once anointed Kings in the Court of Nallur ...?

Arasan's forefathers had ridden on elephants to the royal city. The marks of the elephant chains had scarred some of the palmyrah trees, a few rustling chains, linkless and wasted, remained. The palanquin disintegrated in a corner of the thinnai. Now even the stone elephants on the parapet wall were missing.

"Sellathe, you talk of the past. Are you and mama still living in those times that are finished, gone? We cannot think of coming back to live here for ever and ever. We must wait until our children are grown-up and are on their own. What can we do if we lived here? We must live our lives outside the village. We have other homes now, other lives."

"But mama and I, we have nowhere else."

"That's because mama never wanted to go away completely. Wherever he went he always returned to the village. Now everything that's here is his for as long as he wants. When the time comes perhaps we may return, when we too have no other shelter anywhere else in the world."

"But you will not find mama and myself here, then. You too will be alone as we are, listening to the silence and living in the past. What else do we have?"

"Have all the others gone too – Naganathan, Kulam, Devi?"

"Yes, they are gone."

"And Nagesan, Perambalam, Sivapalan?"

"Gone, all gone."

"Sinnian, Kandian, Sinamma?"

"They are still here. Where else can they go? Like us they have no other home. This is all the land they have, the only home they know. If you ask them to leave the village they will be lost, they will die. Only this land has any meaning for them. What can Kandian do without his palmyrah trees? They're free to do as they want. There is no one for them to serve, no one to obey now that your family is no longer here."

"Is Kurukkal still here?" asked Arasan to stem her flow of words. "I like him to perform an aricchenai in my fathers name."

"Yes, he may be there, but first come and see mama." She would not be pacified.

"Mama is old and feeble now. When your family lived here we could command the respect of the whole village. Now we are left alone. We have nothing. The little money we have is what the relations give us. Nobody comes to help us as they did in the days when your parents were here. Look round you, your parent's land is neglected. The well has not been cleaned for years. The water is green with weeds and moss. It's abounding with frogs, it's not safe to drink the water. Look, it's full of tadpoles and fish; the ul-muttham, is filled with sand, not a plant or blade of grass here; a desert that's what it is."

The distant sound of the koel came from the grove. Parrots swooped and darted about, pillaging the ripe guavas. Looking at the tall trees he thought of the pattams of his youth. "Sellathe, do the village boys still tie those large kites to the trees?" Arasan asked.

How those reed-throated pattams had cried, cried and called to the wind, surging through the huge claw-like fronds of the palmyrah, the huge bird forms that rose far above the grove like guardian deities of the village. The pattams wrestled with the wind and cried to be released but they could soar only within certain limits. All night long the sonorous sound of the wind blew through the throat of the strong reed while Arasan slept feeling the tug of the kite ropes lift and fall, lift and fall, carrying his dreaming body skywards.

Now, looking up at the blue-white sky he saw a few shreds of pale clouds floating above their heads. The sun was coming up, the heat began to burn through the pores. Long floating strands of sunlight wove knots of fire through which the shadows of flying birds were caught and held momentarily.

"No, there is no one left to make those pattams," Sellathe sighed. "We have a home through your father's kindness," she continued. "But of what use is it to us to live alone. You and your brothers must uphold the family traditions. Your family sends money to kurukkal to perform the rituals. But that is not enough. The years come and go. I cannot remember when your father was last here for the Kodiyetham. Come, Arasan, come this year. Take part in the rituals as you have in the past." But now they had all gone their separate ways. The pattam had found its release and drifted over the grove, floating over the endless dunes of sand, to fall where the velvi stones stood crusted with the dried blood of the sacrifice.

"Come Arasan, come this year. Take part in the rituals as you have in the past."

Sellathe refused to accept the changes that had taken place in their lives. She wanted the past to remain as it had once been. The pattam had found its release and drifted over the grove, floating over the endless dunes of sand, to fall where the velvi stones stood crusted with the dried blood of the sacrifice. For Arasan, the kite had fallen, torn from its moorings, when he had been taken to Colombo for his education in a Roman Catholic College. Here, the new rituals were alien to him and listening to the sonorous litanies of the Latin Mass, in place of the rich Sanskrit slokas he had pushed further and further into his consciousness the life of the village. He could not go back to the groves and dunes in a landscape which to him had been instinct and alive with its supernatural and animistic forces.

He had lost the pathway to the ancient temple where the stones glowed like red jewels in the late sun. There was no time left now in his life to replant the flowers and trees in the ul-muttham or drink of the well waters even if the weeds that choked it had been cleaned. The frogs would continue croaking night after night into this vast silence and the carved naga would creep out of the Bhairava temple into the grove wandering among the spirits that dwelt within its light and shade.

We now stood on Thiagarajah Saravanamutthu's land. The space where his old family home had stood was covered with palmyrah trees, that house itself had been completely effaced. Sellathe had been almost moved to tears as she spoke of the past, but now she grew silent as she led us through pathways in the still grove, the green parakeets darting around us. Sellathe led us to her own home. It was a typical house of the village with clay walls built of the rich red earth of Navaly, its roof thatched with fronds of the palmyrah and a thinnai that rose steeply from the garden. The grinding stone lay in a corner, clean, empty upturned earthenpots were piled one on top of the other, some neat bundles of firewood were arranged beside the stones of the hearth. An old man, very fair skinned, a ruddy hue touching its almost milky whiteness and clad in a clean white veshti and shawl reclined on an armchair, reading a book. His fingers, long, white, fine-boned were stained with yellow brown snuff. "Mama, how are you. We have come at last to see you after all these long years." Arasan greeted him with affection, yet a little warily.

Turning to me he said. "This is Ponnambalam mama. I have spoken of him to you."

"Ah, so you are Arasan's wife?" He spoke with great politeness in his somewhat old fashioned, stilted English but his eyes surveyed us wisely, intrusively like those of a hawk, golden, flecked with brown. His mood transitional, changed and abruptly he drew all attention to himself. "Does she know our story?" I looked at him. Sellathe's and his conjointly? Had he expected Arasan to relate it like an epic of their family history? I had heard often enough about the others – the grandparents, the parents, aunts, uncles, cousins, distant or close, of clan pride and wealth, of happiness and tragedy. Where, I wondered did Ponnambalam and Sellathe fit in. No one spoke of them or even mentioned their names in the family circles. It was always – this one did this, or that one did that, something noteworthy or deserving of praise, even the quirks and idiosyncrasies were part of the frieze sculpted out of the monumental memories of the family. Yet it was only Arasan who wanted to remember or cared to do so.

Once Ponnambalam had been called the "Prince of Manipay." He had belonged to one of the best Vellala families; he was fair complexioned, handsome, his features delicately fashioned. He had traveled far and away from the village cutting himself off from the ropes that bound the pattam yet he had missed its wild cry and come back. Reclining in his armchair hour after hour, waking and sleeping he watched the light and darkness pass their wings over the closely growing trees, while he ate the ripe fruit that Sellathe brought him as she wandered about alone in the garden.

He held in his hand a woodapple, ripe, which he had just cracked open. Nothing could be sweeter than a fruit freshly fallen from one of the trees that grew wild in Navaly. The dark richness clung like moist earth to the shell, its fragrance spread into the air which shimmered with heat. The silver light struck hard against the black fronds and a slight wind rustled through them.

"Arasan, you didn't write. Why didn't you answer our last letter?" Arasan could say nothing.

"We wanted help to build this house. Everybody helped, but you." Arasan remained silent yet he had been so fond of Ponnambalam mama.

"You didn't even answer the letter." I remembered.

"Arasan, who are these people?" I had asked as he read the closely written sheets of yellowing paper.

"Relations, distant relations."

"Won't you help them?"

"Yes, yes, I must." But he had somehow forgotten.

Ponnambalam had not forgotten. "We have built this house on your father's land."

Fifty years ago, Sellathe and Ponnambalam had been married. He had come from his village in a grand procession, garlanded and perfumed, in fine silk, his veshti and shawl gold-bordered. The silk of his clothes so sheer and fine that the golden tint of his complexion gleamed through its transparency. He was accompanied by relations, musicians and a whole retinue of people. The tholan had gone to meet him on the way. Nila-pavadai had been spread on the route along which his carriage had passed. On the threshold of the houses kumbum had been placed to welcome him. His pure white, gold bordered turban flickered like a white wing in the sunlight.

He had been welcomed and at the auspicious hour he approached the manaverai. The flame of the sacred yaham had been kindled and was burning with a steady flame. In the bedroom, Arasan's mother and the relatives were dressing the bride. They were whispering to each other. "Ponnambalam has been drinking." Sellathe heard them. She began to cry as they wound the flowers about her hair and draped the stiff folds of the silk sari on her. She cried and cried. "I cannot go with him," she told Arasan's mother.

"Thangatchchie, do not worry. He will change when he is married. He is young. He has had too much money. He will settle down. Don't worry. He's a bit wild now but it will soon be over," Thayalnayaki had consoled. At any rate such scandals as changing one's mind just before the marriage ceremonies could not be permitted in the little village of Navaly. Sellathe had been bathed by all the staid married relations, in milk and water, and the crimson silk sari draped on her body, her hair sleekly oiled and plaited was heavy with jasmine flowers. The womenfolk stood round her like a strong wall through which she could not break through. Soon she too would be one of them, bathing and dressing brides, coming forward and taking her rightful place among them at all the functions and ceremonies. She could not so easily forfeit all this now.

"I will go then," she said reluctantly. "What else can I do, where else can I go? I will be too ashamed to live if I do not accept him now." All the friends and relations had arrived for the marriage ceremonies. The Brahmin priests were preparing to perform the rituals, the musicians were playing the nadhesweran and thavil. Sellathe stepped down firmly from the manaverai and went round the yaham three times with her head bowed, the picture of a traditional Hindu bride. But all eyes were on Ponnambalam. His face flushed, the red flickering flame from the sacred yaham, reflected in his eyes like twin snakes, as groping with the clasp of the thalikoddy he fixed it round her neck.

Soon after the marriage he had gone through whatever money or land she had. Piece by piece he had pawned or sold the jewelry she had brought with her when she had married him. It went to replenish the toddy in the pla, wrought of dried palmyrah leaf, which was the sweetest nectar to him. Now, looking at her I noticed that she no longer wore her thalikody. All they had was each other. She didn't need a thalikoddy. Nothing could undo the clasp he had welded so closely round her neck on the day of their marriage. They had no children, her possessions were few, they had neither land nor wealth yet neither would abandon the other.

For several years Ponnambalam had hardly done a stroke of work. Why should he be overambitious? His relations, would always support him at the worst. Sellathe would never leave him. "And how can I keep even the jobs I get," he would say. "This old athe is so jealous of me. When I was teaching in that little school, the job which your father got for me, athe was always peeping over the wall to see what I was upto. She was so jealous of those pupils of mine. Of course the principal said that I was not concentrating on my work. How could I? I was restless, disturbed, one eye on the book, another on the pupils. I had to have a third eye for athe. I didn't know when her head would pop over that wall to glare balefully at me. Of course I had to go.

"And I was working in the Insurance firm of that fine Englishman, Mr. White. How polite he was to me. Always wishing me good morning or good evening. I kept accounts for him. Ah, I cannot forget him in his white starched suit, collar and tie. That job too your father got for me. Yes, yes, I stayed with that firm for some years and then and then, your athe wanted to come back to Navaly and to what? It was useless. All of you were preparing to go away."

Through those long evenings after drinking toddy Ponnambalam would rant and rave against the relations who had helped him. Sellathe had crouched in a corner listening to him without a murmur.

"Why did I marry this woman? With my looks, my birth, my talents, I could have had the pick of the best families and they would have been proud to have had me as a son-in-law. I could have had a bigger dowry too. You people grudge me even a corner in your house. You put up with me unwillingly yet you have so many empty rooms in your houses. Just a corner for Sellathe and for myself. Do not grudge it. When I have my own house one day, I will treat you to the best I have. In the meantime we must dwell on the fringes of your prosperity and choke on the rice we eat from you."

Sellathe in her resigned fashion listened to all these tirades. Taking a betel leaf from the brass thattu she meticulously placed on it slivers of arecanut, a dab of chunam and spices, folding it neatly into a chew as if she were packing away her thoughts beyond sight. As she put it into her mouth, she ruminated. When he was tired out, he would sleep although Sellathe would stay awake long after the rest of the household had gone to bed. Through the small barred windows of the stone house night sounds would filter in, the whirring of crickets, the frogs from the well and the sound of falling fruits ravaged by night marauders. Her thoughts wavered as she recounted his monologues yet she would never leave him. She had grown attached to him. She felt affection, fondness for him. Although she lived the life of a poor relation she had a place however insignificant among the rest of the married ladies. She had grown strong too. She would survive. A life such as her's left no room for weakness of spirit. So she would rise early and bring hot coffee in a lotah for Ponnambalam and rub his head with lime and oil, wash his veshtis for him and somehow contrive to get him his drink of toddy in the evening.

The years passed and the family house was empty yet it was

she who most fiercely wished to preserve the family traditions on the family property, in the temple, in the village, lording it over Manonmani, Sinnian, Kandian and the others whom she considered lesser beings in the social hierarchy. She hadn't wanted Arasan to have even a cup of tea in Manonmani's house. She and she alone wanted to take Arasan round the family property to show him all that belonged to the brothers and sisters, walking through pathways that led in so many directions on the divided land.

Yet, although Ponnambalam was irresponsible he was charming and kindhearted too. He was perhaps too innocent and guileless, possessing none of the rapacious ambition of those who were the go-getters in life. He felt that his birth, his looks, his charm entitled him to a life of ease and comfort. He did not want to work hard for these things, after all, his tastes were simple. When he had whisky he drank it. When he didn't have that, he contented himself with toddy. When he worked for the Englishmen in the Insurance firm he wore starched white suits and put on polished shoes. When he was in the village he wore a simple cotton veshti. Sellathe however always remained the same. The somber mate to the brilliant chameleon.

Whenever he had a little money to spare from his toddy drinking he would buy fresh prawns from the fisherman who brought villarkutti and other varieties of fish. He would come out with his little clay chatti and buy the fresh prawns. "Just one more, just another prawn," he would say persuasively to the fisherman. The prawns he would grind finely to make savory cutlets for Arasan and his brothers. When he was short of money he would shoot the wild pigeons that flew about so abundantly in the grove and make pigeon pie.

Now lying stretched out on the armchair he seemed content enough to read from the Ramayana and eat ripe woodapple, sleeping idly in the sun, awakening and listening to the slight yet sharp thud of the green mangoes and little kurumbettis as they fell throughout the day, the burnished polished skins a tender yellow green. I wondered who brought him his toddy now in the brimming pla. Who was there now to command Kandian to bring it to his feet, unless he did it out of courtesy and kindliness for the raffish old man. The shadows played on Sellathe's neck softening the gaunt hollows and jutting bones where the heavy thalikody had rested. Her neck was bare, the gold had long been spent but the clasp which Ponnambalam had so unsteadily fixed seemed invisible, unyieldingly molded into her skin.

Lost in his dreams he lay there sleeping and waking savoring the pleasures of being alive. The mango trees around him season after season sprouted blossoms, the fruits grew ripe and hung in pendant clusters from the branches, oil oozed from the gingelly seeds crushed in the chekku. Who would continue to fill it with seed and gather the oil. Only Kandian was left to tap the palmyrah flower and fill the pots with their nectar. Ponnambalam charmingly continued to live off his relations as he had always done but he was now left alone to rule over those wide demesnes. But power he did not possess, to wield over a single human being. He did not feel its sting as much as Sellathe did. She felt the loss of power more than anyone else. Ponnambalam had asked for much less from life. It was Sellathe who was avid for power. She bemoaned the passing of the old times.

"When your mother was here, how many people served your family. Now there is no one to even draw water from the well, no one to renew the fences, no one to care for your fields and gather the harvest or even pluck the fruits. I pick up what I can from the garden. Weeds have sprung up round the walawu. Nagalingam is too old to clean the well. The ul-muttham is filled with sand. The neighbors' goats and cattle wander in through the broken fences. We can't even plant a coconut palm. The animals destroy the plants as soon as they start sprouting. Do you remember your family guru, Yogaswamy? When he was alive you had his blessing."

We were sitting on the few available chairs on the thinnai. Sellathe had kindled a fire to boil water for tea. The wood smoke rose in acrid gusts as she blew at it to make the fire burn.

She took some tumblers out of a basket and also brought out several thosais.

"Take, children, take and eat," she offered generously. "Eat the thosai. Are you not hungry, children. Here, take the white coconut sambol."

Ponnambalam mama held out one of the cracked halves of his woodapple. "Children take it, share it between the two of you. It's sweet and ripe. Your father will tell you how many he ate as a child but then with a stone he could very skilfully bring down the ripest fruit, I don't know how he spotted them. I think he could smell them from the top-most branch. Arasan you will bring me the ripe ones when you come here again, won't you? Now its only what athe gathers for me that I must be content with. Ah, well, I have my pla of toddy to look forward to occasionally. Although Kandian must be reminded of his duties or he will finish a whole pot by himself. Now children take the woodapple at least."

"No, mama. You eat the woodapple. We don't want any. Kandathe has given us a lot of thosai too. We brought them for our lunch from Keerimalai."

"But we must be careful when we eat them," Devasundari said. "Sometimes we find goat hair in her thosai." "Ah, you will not find goat hairs in your athe's thosai. Soft and fine they are" Ponnambalam spoke proudly of his wife's food.

All Ponnambalam and Selathe had now was this wide thinnai and a small room, a clay hut which after their death would fall apart and become part of the earth. Inside the one little room there was an old couch spread with a patchwork quilt for Ponnambalam to sleep on. Thick, heavy mats were rolled up and suspended by rope from the roof. In one corner of the thinnai was placed a basket of margosa seeds from which oil could be crushed in a small hand-press. Selathe had another basket with a few old saris.

Once Ponnambalam had been made caretaker of a house in Manipay. Every evening he would go to the toddy grove to drink his brimming pla of toddy – on credit – the debt grew and grew. His supplier became impatient and began to demand his toddy money. But how could Ponnambalam ever pay it back? There was nothing more of Sellathe's to sell. Ponnambalam was at his wits end. But he was never at a loss for long. Every night the neighbors heard the sound of tapping and breaking. They became suspicious and informed the owner of the house of the mysterious goings-on there. One night he surprised Ponnambalam. Carrying his lantern through the dark garden he had knocked on the door. There he stood among the strewn bricks looking only slightly perturbed at the interruption.

"Ah, my friend, it is late. Were you restless? Couldn't you sleep? Do you want to fetch the Parihari? You shouldn't walk alone through the garden at night what with reptiles, scorpions, who knows what."

Ponnambalam had been taking apart the walls, brick by brick, to sell to his creditor. The man was building a new house for himself out of the Vellala structure. What shocked his relations most was not the fact that he was stealing the bricks but that he was giving them all away without a conscience, without a thought for his clan. The house was a symbol of the Vellala clan structure and here was Ponnambalam taking it apart; that he too was being displaced did not matter to him. He would always find a place to live in. He had never been shelterless, there was always a niche for him somewhere. He lay now, reclining on the armchair submissive and saint-like but still with that gleam in his eyes, ever so slight, of wicked amusement. While Sellathe only cared about maintaining their respect in the village he kept talking about the money he needed to live, of how little he had of it for his creature comforts and chuckling over a rather risqué story of a distant cousin of his who had been chased by the police for some misdemeanor in the past. The young fellow had run from garden to garden jumping over or creeping through pottu in the palmyrah fences hotly pursued by the law. Ponnambalam had lain on his armchair egging him on and then he had deliberately misled the police. And today, this very person was abroad, prosperous, rich, a staid and respectable citizen of the country, sending Ponnabalam money for his needs. "Bring Naganathan's letter and read it to Arasan," he told Sellathe. "Yes, he has not forgotten me. Last month he sent me ten pounds." He looked at Arasan from the corners of his eyes. His tone suddenly changed and became suffused with self-pity. He continued his monologue, Sellathe listening silently.

"I am a sick man now. There is only this old athe to look after me. Sometimes I get a little money from here and there but how could it be sufficient for us to live on?"

Arasan was silent. Ponnambalam had managed to live through his life with the minimum of effort. He had done only the things that gave him pleasure. When he was young he had helped to make those enormous man-sized pattams which rifted the air with sound. The kite was moored to its tree firmly although it followed the pathways of the wind. He had broken away from the strong rope. He had seen the world until spent and weary he had come back to rest in the grove. Here, he now enjoyed the bounty of the land; all these acres rich in palmyrah and fruit trees were his alone. He lived on Thiagarajah's land but no one came to live here permanently. They had all migrated to the city or gone abroad. The garden yielded its first fruits to him, the hearth would never be cold for there was plenty of firewood to be collected from the grove.

"Come Arasan, let us go and look at your old home. Your children must see where your father grew up but don't imagine it is what it was like in the past."

"Good bye, mama. We will come again to see you."

Ponnambalam mama leant back on the armchair. Already his eyes were closing, the empty shells of the woodapple had fallen on the ground.

"Good bye, Arasan, good bye to all of you, children, next time you come we will listen to the vinkoovel. Now your father is impatient to go but when you return we will make a pattam larger and greater and when you sleep at night in your father's house you will hear it humming through its reed throat. You will see it like a great dark bird of night; it will drown the sound of the frogs croaking and you will dream that you are sailing through the darkness over the groves and dunes where Amman and Bhaivara will always be a presence."

"We will open the doors and sweep out the floors, arrange the furniture. Nagalingam can clean out the well. Sellachchi can come and cook for you all," said Sellathe.

"But come, let us see the family house first." We walked across the land strewn with fallen palmyrah fruit and margosa flowers. Arasan could see no familiar landmarks. There wasn't a sign of the lotus pool nor the pomegranate tree. In the ul-muttham, piles of silvery white sand glinted in the strong white sunlight. The dunes seemed to be creeping closer to the house. Faint marks of wind-drifting leaves and twigs had traced their patterns on it. Pillars of coconut wood upheld the roof with its fine brown speckled grain. There were two small bedrooms, the doors deeply carved with wreaths of flowers and leaves. Heavy brass keys hung from the keyholes. They would hardly turn in the locks.

"Your grandfather's pettagams, Arasan." They had once contained the family wealth.

"What is in them, Sellathe?" Arasan asked idly.

"Your mother's brass and copper vessels, the kuththuvillakku, all the things that no one uses any longer. Come, I will take you to see your share of the property."

We left the house, walking through pathways of white sand until we came to the fenced off section where Kandian lived. He stood in the garden among the palmyrah trees. It was cool in the shade cast by the great black fronds. His wiry body glistened with the same sheen that the palmyrah fruit possessed. His face beamed at Arasan and even while he greeted him he held out his knife, the knife with which he severed the palmyrah flower, it's blade glittering sharply in the sunlight. His body was almost hidden by the shadows of the fronds yet the glittering knife seemed to sever the shadows, parting then with a silver tongue.

"Ah, thambi, after how many years do I see you. And what a changed person you are. Didn't you hear about my brother Sinnian? He died recently. He fell from the tree when he climbed to catch wild parrots and that was the end of him. Now his two daughters are left without a father. What is to become of them?"

The light danced on the shining blade with which he slit the palmyrah flower.

"Rasa, the toddy is now all over or I would have offered you some. Do you remember the fresh nectar you drank as a child from the flowers I tapped? Now I am growing old and I struggle to come to the surface but I drown like a bee in my own honey."

"Kandian, I will come and see you again. The next time I return I will come early to take the first drink from your pot of toddy. Keep a fresh pla for me."

"Rasa, are you sure that you will return? Come soon then. Don't wait till the rainy season. Come when the nectar of the flower is at its sweetest. Do not wait until it is too late, you will find I am not here and that my pots are empty."

"I will return, Kandian. Come, Sellathe, we must go back. We must return to Keerimalai before dark," said Arasan. They began to retrace their steps. Sellathe pointed to the carved cobra on the stone tablet in the Bhairava temple.

"See Parvathi, see Devasundari. Many years ago your grandfather had this cobra carved for the temple." The naga head flared out of the sculptured stone, glittering black, its hood a dark outspread flower, glinting with silver motes, powerful, potent.

Sellathe bent low touching the folds of the cobra and the outspread hood. Its power seemed to enfold her in its coils at once comforting and protective.

"You will return, Arasan?" She asked. "If you do, mama and I can hear the vinkoovel again. Now the nights are lonely with only the trees around us and the wild birds and frogs croaking from the kerny. Kurukkal too will be happy when you come to the temple once again for the poojas every evening. After all it was your father who gave his land for the temple veedhi. If you stay long enough we can start planting the ulmuttham again with flowers."

"Athe, athe, we must go now. It is growing so late." Sellathe, Kandian and some of the village folk came in a small procession to the bus stand by the temple to see us off. Kandian was drunk with toddy, the toddy which he himself had tapped from the flower, filling the clay pots brimful. Now that he was no longer standing on the property of the Vellala family, he flaunted himself boldly, flourishing his toddy tapping knife and talking loudly.

"Ah, now we are free. The old days are over and done with. Why should we continue to follow the old customs and traditions of our forefather to serve you Vellalas. Let us see who will carry your biers in the future. You will have to carry them yourselves. Ha, we are free, free, free."

All this he said looking in the direction of Sellathe. He bore no rancor towards Arasan. She was discomfited. Her proud hand had pointed to the carved naga in the temple. It was not the juice of the toddy that dripped from its flickering blade. It was venom. Sellathe's neck bared itself to him empty of its thalikoddy, within its hollows nestled a shadow like the coiled naga with its flowering hood poised to strike.

"Rasa," Kandian said "Who can now tell us we should do this, we should do that? We obeyed your father. My father obeyed your grandparents. We have lived here for centuries. Where else are we to go? Who are we to serve now that your father and his sons are no longer here."

"We are here. We remain," murmured Sellathe. "And what good is that? If Arasan thambi returns I will bring him the full pot of toddy and the fruit he loved as a child. I will do that out of respect for his family. But he will go away. Will he ever return, or his children? I am too old to make a pattam for them and even if I do, will my arms be strong enough to hold the ropes which bind them to the tree?"

Kandian's knife flashed like the naga head poised for destruction.

"Hush, Kandian, don't talk so loud. The police will take you away." She spoke childishly. Pointing his knife towards her as if he were preparing to slit the palmyrah flower, he laughed and laughed and said, "Me? Take me away? No, it is you rather who will be taken away...."

Ponnambalam mama was safe in the grove dozing in his armchair, the margosa flowers falling silently around him, lying so quietly in his half sleep, drifting into death, the half-eaten woodapple in his hands which were as delicate and fragile as the ribs of an ivory fan.

"Thambi," she appealed, "Navaly is no longer what it was like when you were a child here many years ago." Sellathe was almost in tears. She turned away unable to speak.

In this silence, the bus arrived.

"We are going, Sellathe. Come and spend the day with us at Keerimalai. Bring mama along too."

We got into the bus. It started off. We kept looking back at the little group standing forlornly outside the half-open gateway, in the shade of the tamarind tree.

Kandian was still gesticulating violently at Sellathe. His knife, sharp-bladed flashed in the sun and Arasan felt himself drowning. Drowning in the nectar which Kandian had so often given him, fresh from the tree. But the aftermath of its remembrance was now bitter on his tongue.

THE PREDICTION

To reach Pella, we drove, Dawoo (who was from Taiwan and who continued his own immigrant journeys in these regions) and I, in a Chevrolet van along miles and miles of lonely road and woods, reminders of the traditional hunting grounds of the displaced tribes of the Sioux Indians. Cornfields glowed in a sheet of straight-stalked gold, the ripening corn emerging from the bleached white sheaths. Occasionally the carcass of some wild dead animal, perhaps a possum or skunk that had wandered out of the woods to cross onto the other side of the road, lay before us, run over and killed. The thick pelt, inert and limp, a mound of dead fur slung across a highway. The woods were russet and gold with burnished fall leaves.

As we were nearing Pella, names appeared on signboards, names that suggested Dutch colonization. Suddenly, the little township confronted my eyes as if from nowhere. The name that recurred on the signboard was to me yet another landmark from the history of another era. "Veenstra." "Vote for Veenstra." "Veenstra for Supervisor." Veenstra was an invisible presence but names like his dominated the scene of the island from which I came – Van Eyck, Jansz, Van Langenberg, Van Gramberg, de Woolf, Van der Graaf and a host of others. Echoes traveled through my mind, echoes which bore their own dissonances. Veenstra's shadowy ancestry, like mine must have traveled from the polder lands, but his ship, his voyage, his sea route, had been in a different direction. My great great grandfather, Adriaan Jansz had crossed the Oceanus Orientalis tempted by the desire for his own advancement. His imagination and his needs, fired by the fables of the East and the opportunities for acquiring wealth. Listening to narratives of the experiences brought back to Holland by adventurers and seamen like Guyon le Fort and Joris van Spilbergen.

Veenstra's ancestors and the Dutchmen who had traveled thousands of miles in their covered wagons had sought a different kind of wealth, the acres and acres of virgin land, flat, like the polder country with horizons that extended into limitless space. There was thick forest, still abounding with the game which the Indian tribes had hunted, forests with an abundance of rich timbers and fields of Indian corn. For the greater part however, the virgin forest had been cleared and homesteads set up in this gigantic spread of land where the cornfields were ploughed, sown, harvested and threshed by the huge Harvest Combines. Machines which devoured the land. This land could now contain the amplitude of families, gable-topped houses, kirks and stores. Landmarks of a new heritage. Maple sap was gathered to make syrup for pannekokjes and suikerbrod.

On the land taken over by his forebears Veenstra now raised hogs, cattle, poultry and grew corn. My thoughts went back to that eighteenth century ancestor, Adriaan Jansz, who had become part of a vast, exploitative machinery, the Oost Indische Compagnie. A Company that had as its main objectives firstly, to be the sole masters of Ceylon "to the exclusion of all other nations." Secondly, it was responsible for the collection of the products in particular and the trade in general in "All stations and comptoirs," according to the memoirs of Jan Schreuder, Governor of Ceylon.

How endlessly the processions of the people of the island had borne "their baskets of tribute, binding the cinnamon bales, paying their taxes and rents" while the Dutch ambassadors had wooed the king of Kandy with an exotic menagerie of animals, among which were Arabian horses and the white tiger. Trade and barter existed for the profit of the colonizer. Treaties were made and boundaries defined for the extension of power.

A different kind of history must now be written by their progenitors. Here, in the New World, the lonely spirits of the Sioux, of Hawk Eye, of all the displaced tribes still wandered, their burial grounds hidden in the woods where the wild deer herds dwelt. Deer herds that soon would feel gun shot when the closed season was over and the hunters came in search of game. Here in these temperate climes, cool airs blowing across his face, Veenstra and his kind maintained a language and traditions until new settlers came to live in their midst from the outside world. My own ancestor had lived in the Fort of Galle beside the Indian Ocean. Here Veenstra was landlocked.

What was I doing here, traveling in this direction, to reach an unknown destination. Almost two hundred years after Adriaan Jansz began laying the foundations of his family in the Dutch fortress of Galle, this visit was arranged for me at Pella, another Dutch Colony in the mid-west of America. I was on an International Writers Fellowship at the University of Iowa in 1991. The Director and the others who were in charge of the program thought that I would be interested in seeing what Dutch colonization had done in that part of the New World. I was to have a glimpse into the era of Dutch emigrant experience. It had been a different kind of colonization in Pella unlike that which had taken place in the island of Ceylon. There, battles of great bloodshed and carnage had taken place in the process of ousting the Portuguese power which had been entrenched in the forts of the maritime provinces for over a century. Whatever it was, the original inhabitants of both colonies had suffered displacement within the context of colonial conquest. I was curious about my journey into the hinterland and prepared myself to read poems which dealt with my own search for an identity that I had inherited, one imposed upon me historically and not from choice.

I read my poetry to my audience. What stirred them most were my political poems not those that belonged to a remote period of colonization. Identity was not a burning question at Pella. After the reading, Robyn Martin took me to the Dutch Bakery which was famous for its cakes and pastries. It was fragrant with the smells of baking. The glass-fronted shelves were piled with baskets and platters of Dutch crullers, buttery and crumbly, redolent with the fragrance of rich almond paste. My thoughts went back to my childhood, to the comforts of home, relations, friendship. At Christmas time, the breudhers baked in their fluted pans eaten with fresh butter and Edam cheese, bolo fiado, fougetti, love cake and pastole, savory meat patties. Food was also remembrance, of recipes handed like genealogies down the line. Identity embodied in their flavors. A childhood over and done with. Memories clung like crumbs of flaky pastry to the fingers. A lingering touch on the tongue and lip.

I thought of my kith and kin and their emigration to other lands, of the letters they wrote to me of their settling into a new life; of the abundance of dried fruit marinating in brandy for the Christmas cake; the lamprais which tried to retain a flavor of the past, yet losing something distinctive in the process of being baked in foil, rather than in plantain leaf. There was a special fragrance in that leaf which itself became impregnated with the flavor of fricadels, fried ash plantain curry, lamprais curry, blachan and the coconut milk that enveloped the cooked rice as it gradually began to assimilate the spices and meats, for the lamprais curry was an amalgam of mutton or beef, chicken, pork, vegetables and dried roasted shrimp. My people who had emigrated would themselves often send Christmas parcels of preserved cherries, raisins, sultanas, currants, candied peel or even Christmas cake and love cake to far away cousins in the New World from the distant Antipodes. Flavors and tastes were now compounded of my thought and imagination. So, in the mixing of the ingredients and their preparation there would always remain a mingling of memory and the felt experiences of the past. In the mixing and baking, the traditional cake too, tasted of part of the emigrant experience and that longing and nostalgia for the country of their birth.

Remembrance was now preserved in the contents of those packages that came from Australia. The flavor of the new continent became part of the flavor of the island which they had known before their departure. When some of my relations left after their vacations in the island, they would take lamprais packets which they would microwave in Canada and Australia. Wherever they went the Burgher caterers had carried on their individual skills, making stringhoppers colored with pink and green cochineal, wedding cake, Christmas cake, love cake, breudher, lamprais. The seamstresses sewed wedding gowns and ankle length debutante gowns. Only in the new country they could be more lavish, they could earn more and they could entertain as they had once done in the past. Yet, there was always that hankering for the return, for the seeking out of friends and familiar landscapes in maps of the mind which had long since changed, their well known landmarks effaced.

One day, many years ago, I had visited Mrs. Van Ranzow. Her husband was a descendent of Count Van Ranzow. She was reputed to have a remarkable gift for reading palms and predicting the future, a gift she had either inherited or acquired but which had made her famous in Colombo at the time in the fifties. Gazing into her face with its strong lines, intense and penetrating hawk-like eyes, the haggard beauty of her face became a portrait that would forever be painted on the canvas of imagination and memory. Within her was the gift in the ancient knowledge of humankind.

I was just out of University and still to know which routes to embark on. Errors and miscalculations of navigation had left me stranded on unfriendly islands with the danger of being marooned for life. I wanted to voyage out and had always spent hours reading women travel writers like Freya Stark, Gertrude Bell, Rosita Forbes among others. When I began teaching I peered into volumes past and present of the National Geographic and immersed myself in those journeys and sojourns in Bali, in the Caribbean and in the Amazon jungles. At that stage of my life I had gone back to painting. There were bare spaces on those canvases and in my life that I had to fill with people and landscapes.

"Tell me what you see in the lines of my palm. Can you

foretell my destiny?" Mrs. Van Ranzow scrutinized the tracings on my palm, those lines that marked the routes, crisscrossing, of an unexplored ocean. I believed she would help me to charter my course. I had to prepare myself for the hazards of the voyage. I had still to peruse the old maps on which my forebears had traced their sea routes. Knowledge would come later, of that guilt laden ancestry with its whole load of the burdens of conquest and colonization.

"You will have two paths to choose from, two ways from which you must make your choice. Yes, you will cross the seas. You will always be a traveler." I sat before her like a votary. The moment she had walked out onto the verandah of her little suburban house in Colombo in a kind of trance, like some High Priestess I knew she held the keys to the entire plan of my life. Its scope was as yet unrealized. She would be the cartographer of my sea route, the pilot and navigator of my voyages. It was she who helped me launch my vessel onto the ocean embarking on journeys in blind faith.

Where Mrs. Van Ranzow was concerned, she was here to stay. In the island where her ancestors had been soldiers, coopmen, administrators of the VOC or perhaps soldiers from that famous mercenary regiment of Colonel de Meuron in the seventeenth century. This was a safe harbor for her. She possessed a great gift which she now used to foretell the future. Behind her heavy-lidded eyes dark with their interior knowledge it appeared that she saw all that was hidden from our vision.

I believed her words and went my way. I reached safe harbors, was caught up in storms, shipwrecked and marooned but for the rest of my life, I was to travel. Mrs. Van Ranzow would have told me that there was no other way to charter a destination. Or several of them. I should have searched her out once more to tell her of my own traveler's tales. One day I would perhaps seek out her beginnings for her ancestry too was recorded in the old volumes of the Dutch Burgher Union – where all the beginnings of those genealogies stemming from that conquest still remained.

Our paths diverged. I went my way but I was never to forget the words of the prophetess Van Ranzow. She gave me the sacred mantra which I kept locked up in my heart. I trusted her utterance. I did not even feel I needed a map to guide my voyages. She, that Sybil, was the mystical navigator of my life when I was still to discover the route to any destination. My travels were still to come. I had no stories to tell. I had to cross oceans. I had to reach ports and harbors. I remember how once I had sailed out to a lighthouse. It had a name. Foul Point. On the eastern coast of the island surrounded by jagged rocks and surging waves. I had slept on the ledge of that lighthouse surrounding the tower, under the star filled skies. Feeling the spray touch my body. Tasting brine on my lips. I felt becalmed on the ocean of my life. On the ocean of time. On the horizon a ghostly vessel with tattered sails floundered on the turbulent waves. I could hardly make out the insignia of that invader vessel but I knew somehow, buried in time, were the memories of those ancestors who had landed on the shores of this island and formed their private enclaves. The lighthouse still stands but those strong beams fall on the ocean to guide other vessels. I emerged out of that colonial enclave born into a world where I had to find signposts of my own devising to guide me. Dangers, hazards, risks. Where were the warnings? I did not walk with the saints but I shared their pilgrimages.

The road to Pella brought me to this historical juncture in my life in the heart of this continent. The people who had their settlements here would never change. They did not want to. I was a visitant. A transient. My stay would be brief. Not like those historical emigrants and invaders. I had only the country of myself to return to where no flag of conquest would ever fly. The territory of my uninvaded self. Where I would finally discard that archival documentation from an identity scrawled in heirographics of blood. Nameless. Anonymous. Dismissing the archaic language of that identity, no longer duped by history's forgeries of name and lineage. This was the final truth. The choice of a route. Maneuvering the vessel of myself to voyage out, explore, discover but never, never to lay claim to or acquire territory or set up boundaries. The prophetess Van Ranzow had stayed behind and sent me out. There were no El Dorados anymore to be found. Pella was just another name on a map but a place that had shown me the reality of conquest. And the bitter lessons of displacement of those to whom that land had once belonged.

EXODUS

When they arrived finally, at Chavakachcheri, it was 11 AM nearing midday, the sun already scorching their skins. Mohan's mother-in-law's property now had all the appearance of an oasis with its palmyrah, coconut, tamarind, mango, lime, an oasis in this desert for the footsore, exhausted, disheveled and sick at heart traveler. They had walked endless kilometers without a halt.

Chavakachcheri. The stopover before the next lap of the journey. Hundreds of thousands of refugees. Fleeing from their homes in different parts of the Peninsula. Walking. Walking. Walking. Non stop for the last eighteen hours. Escape. From the military thrust of Forces from the South. From the impending fall of the city. The capital of the Peninsula.

Armies in the past had taken the same route. The soldiers of Chandrabhanu in the thirteenth century with his regiments of Javakas. They had come from the Malayan Peninsula, crossed over, marched through this landscape of white sand dunes into the North Central Province. Began to be involved in the troubled politics of that era.

The Javakas. Perhaps that is how Chavakachcheri got its name.

"It is retribution for what we did to the Muslims perhaps. They too had to leave their homes and flee when the order was given by the militants. Emptied the Peninsula of them. No time to prepare for departure. Like ourselves. That's what some of them think." Mohan's unspoken thoughts. As the exodus begins on this seemingly endless road.

What will the troops from the South encounter? In this city which many of them have never set eyes on before? Ruins. After the bombing and the shelling. Deserted abandoned roads and buildings.

For Mohan, Revathi his wife, their little daughter Rhema and a relative who had accompanied them, Chavakachcheri was the route of the refugees. The temporary stopover. Joining the packed columns of ants whose lives were both expendable and anonymous. Whether they survived or not was of importance only to themselves and their kith and kin. Unarmed. Survivors caught up in the great battle where soon the flag of conquest would fly over the terrain. Set up in the deserted capital as the armies from the South milled round its standard. Dividing a divided people still further? Or to unify them? The paradoxes were there for them to contemplate as they walked, step by measured step. Hour by hour.

"Water, water, water," Rhema had constantly called out. Where could they stop for water? If they moved out of the column even for a moment, how could they step into place again? The gaps filled within an instant.

How had the Javanese army survived that march in that far away time? What weapons did they carry? Blowpipes? Arrows with poisoned barbs? And water to quench their thirst? Did they find the waters in the wells of the Peninsula sweet or bitter?

Mohan thought of the waters of Marah when the Israelites began their journey through the wilderness. Bitter waters made sweet by the tree that was cast into it. To the man who lived in the Peninsula, the waters from his well tasted sweet, tasted of the mineral-filled soil of his land. And what about the commissariat of those Javaka troops? Did they get their provender from those isolated habitations they passed through along the way? They must have felt thirst in that long march through the arid plains. Did the soldiers murmur to their commandant or generals and say as the Israelites to Moses.

"What shall we drink? What shall we drink?"

Mohan felt his daughter's suffering. She was only two years

old. In all the haste of departure, his wife distraught, taking whatever they could of the money they had at hand, no one had thought of water. Revathi, his cousin Padmini, he himself were prepared to endure all things in order to keep moving, moving, moving away from the oncoming armies and finally, out of the Peninsula to the South where his mother and brother lived. They had made their journey earlier before the military campaign to take over the entire Peninsula, had begun, part by part. If the family could make the crossing through the Kilaly lagoon by boat, and reach Vavuniya, they could plan how to travel to the South.

"Water, appah, water, water."

"Have patience, my daughter, soon we will reach your grandmother's home. You can have food, water, a bath and sleep peacefully there."

"What of the troops?" Mohan thought. Fighting their way, every inch of the way ... attack, defence ... meant death, mortal wounds, limbs blasted by landmines ... both sides ... enemies ... the guerrillas, the Security Forces ... don't they long for water too? Marching endlessly on those routes is a different direction to ours ... do they not long for water from their wells in the South?

Mohan felt he could endure hunger, thirst, exhaustion but looking upon the faces of his wife, of his child, of his cousin, he felt a surge of pity for them observing their taut expressions, the older women summoning the will to survive the long trek. His shirt clung to his body, wringing wet with sweat. He thought of the oil of the sesame seed massaged into his limbs on a hot, sunny morning in his home at Mirusuvil and the paste of soap nut lathering his body before the well water, bucket alter bucket was poured on him making his skin silky smooth. Cool. That was in the past and already receding so rapidly from his mind.

This obsession with thirst. Parched throats. Even the wetness of his shirt was a slight comfort to him. He remembered the Old Testament readings in the church. Elim. Yes, Elim. Twelve wells of water and threescore and ten palm trees. His mother-in-law's home would be the oasis when they finally got there. Even if it were a temporary oasis, it would be a resting-place for them. Unlike the hundreds and thousands of other travelers. The old. The sick. The women and children. Walking. Just keep going. On and on. Mohan felt hardly human. The march had begun the previous evening at six o'clock. In the gathering dusk. The hour at which his daughter would have her evening meal. Listen to stories. And later, prepare for bed. Instead they were out on the road. Walking. Crawling. For mile upon mile. Stumbling. Faltering. Pausing. Unable to take even one step for half an hour at a time. Just standing still until he felt the movement begin almost imperceptibly, like a shudder running through the phalanx of bodies each one supporting the weakness of the other. Tottering against the spent body of the other. Hear the hissing breath. The stifled sigh. The silent wail. Sharing an intimacy almost lethal in its closeness. They had to obey the orders of the militants to move out of their homes. Out of the city and out of the surrounding villages. And why? Rumors were rampant. The Security Forces from the South were advancing. They would soon converge on the city. A people imprisoned within the fears of those whom they saw as the "enemy." They were uncertain of their fate if they were to remain behind. That's where rumor came in. They felt they had no hope left except in escape. They had known military occupations of the recent past. They were with this one alternative. Vacate their homes, leave the Peninsula. Go where then? Into the wilderness?

There was hardly any time to take practical measures for this hurried emptying of the city. Would the capital fall to the invading armies? With no one to defend or resist its capitulation? The guerrillas would not bear the white flag of truce. Nor would there be resistance. No siege either. But to each of them, beleaguered souls, it would be the capitulation of the self. To forces, to orders that no one could countermand. Each man, each woman was a ghost town within, hollow, painful, empty and broken. There was no need of a white flag for this capitulation. For those who had already lost their freedom.

This new bondage would not matter. When if ever would they come out whole? Who would lead them through the wilderness and out again? Could they ever return to their homes? Retrace steps through memory, through the deafening sounds of gun fire, bursting shells and artillery into a vast and echoless space of silence. Where the shattered conch splintered, scattered in fragments with no longer a message to summon or herald the penitent or the seeker of the gods. The temple shrouded in a pall of darkness until the flares of the conqueror fell upon the walls and the ancient pujaris with trembling hands held the pooja trays, the coconuts split, spilling their precious liquid on the lingam in the inner sanctum.

Water, water, water. How precious each drop to these staunch columns that would not fall, if they could help it but keep going, on and on.

The militants had decided that they would not stay on to do battle in the capital but they had left it heavily mined. Even the dwellings of the populace had been mined. The sound of bursting shells still echoed in their ears. How could they say, "We do not want to go. We want to remain." "Leave immediately. This is your only chance to move out before we blow up the main bridge. We will help ferry you across the Kilaly lagoon. Provision will be made for you in Killinochchi in the Wanni area."

How many of them would reach that destination? There was both fear and division in their minds. Torn apart by the orders to leave their homes. Never perhaps to return. Who would give them assurance that they would ever reach the promised land? They followed each other, those in front assuming leadership. Into the wilderness. To be fed with manna and locusts. Already they felt the pangs of hunger, thirst, cold and wet, sun and dew. Rain. Exhaustion. All this lay ahead of them. Succumb on the way. Would the very old and sick be able to endure the journey, thought Mohan. Streaming out on to the main arterial road, tightly packed columns of frightened, fearful, panic stricken people. "How long can we remain human?" Mohan conjectured. His wife spoke not a word. Her anxieties were centered entirely on the child, but his thoughts whirled round his head. "Have we betrayed ourselves or have we been betrayed? By whom has this betrayal been engineered? All we can observe now is the politics of escape and survival. Yes, that's all. Summon within ourselves all our strength or we will perish. A wrong move. A miscalculated step. A cry of alarm. Would only result in a wild stampede and worse onslaught than either being attacked or having to defend ourselves without arms. Loss of life at any rate was inevitable. Suffocation. Asphyxiation. No escape if you were caught in the middle and your legs gave way as you stooped to pick up something when the momentum, slow and labored as it was, got going. Enormous reserves of self discipline were needed to ensure that each one came out of this alive...."

"Is there any point in counting the hours already spent before we reach Chavakachcheri?" The happenings of the day before unreeled themselves, montaged in Mohan's mind.

On the road from 5 PM to 11 AM the next day. Journey to the main city from our house on its outskirts. Then take the route leading out of the city. A journey counted in steps. Placing one foot before the other with the greatest deliberation. A sea of heads on the road. The feelings of uncertainty. Of insecurity. Not knowing what would happen next. Impelled onto this road. Why? Unsure. Unsure. Once the victorious troops from the South reached the capital what would happen to us. One part of their mission accomplished. Loss of life on their side too.... At whose mercy would we be left? The militant cadres had already begun their retreat. Their families had begun moving out of the city earlier. In vehicles. We had to go on foot. What transport was available would never be able to accommodate the surging crowds.

What could I do as I walked but review my life. Hardship, vicissitudes I had known. At that moment of departure there was very little turmoil in my own mind about what could happen to me ... my wife however had been panic stricken. Leaving her home. Taking the child with us. Being responsible for a relative whose husband was abroad. As for myself, life had never been easy, beginning from my childhood days with the loss of my father at a very early age. I had friends who belonged to mixed ethnic groups. Our relationships had never been marred by strife or dissension. I could converse in the language of the majority Sinhala ethnic community too whenever the occasion demanded. I never felt myself a person apart from the mainstream of humanity. Remember that day. We all thought it was an epoch making moment when that helicopter from the South had landed on our terrain in the Peninsula. Those arbiters of peace had stepped out of it, the representatives of the new government that had come into power. The crowds had surged forward in thousands to greet them, welcome them. To garland them, and fling roses at them. "Peace, peace, we want peace," was what they all cried out with one voice. And for our people, the chance to live in dignity, with acceptance among the others. Not to be thought of as the enemy. How then had we come to this? Those self same crowds, hundreds and thousands of us, fleeing – without supplies of food or water or any kind of medical supplies, only the eventuality of being hurt or fainting or just collapsing. April the 19th 1995 had been the day of the cease-fire. The Joint Services assault and Tiger resistance coincided to the day with its violation in which Tiger frogmen destroyed two naval ships in the Eastern part of the island, in Trincomalee without warning of cease-fire termination. Hostilities had recommenced. Operation Sunrise 1, had begun. And these very crowds that had greeted the peacemakers were now part of this mass exodus. Paradoxical indeed. The militant spokesman had spoken of the government's "Secret Agenda." The implications were that the militants who had been in power after creating their de facto state would be ousted and destroyed.

The North would then come under military rule. We were the ordinary citizens caught in-between in this war which had been raging for over twelve years. Did our lives matter to anyone, Mohan wondered. We were all caught up in the violent struggle for a separate state, for a separate homeland. No one could answer a single question about our future. We trod the dust. The sooner one footprint was left, it was effaced by that of the other and the other. I wondered what the feeling of the last column, the stragglers were as we moved on. At least they had the freedom of not having the whole weight of humankind pressing down upon their shoulders, allowing the wind to mingle with their breath yet choking on the dust blown up by the marching columns. When the rain began to fall they were soaked to the skin. Drenched. Trudging through rutted mud tracks.

The militants had fought too hard and too long to gain the power they held. No one would be allowed to wrest that power. In making the decision not to stay back and fight, to the finish – they turned to a fresh alternative, the move to the Wanni regions. Their new capital to be Killinochchi. They had begun stripping the asbestos roofing to provide temporary housing for the refugees.

The Wanni regions – never thought we would have to move there – had it's own history. The place where semi-independent chiefs had held sway during the successive wars of invasions.

In the seventeenth century, Maria Sembatte, the Wanninchee had resisted the Dutch power. A courageous woman. Strong in spirit. She was taken away as a prisoner by the Dutch. Kept in captivity in the Dutch Fort of Colombo. Plenty of young women like her fighting now for the Cause. The martial feminists belong to the Tiger cadres – Sea Tigers – suicide bombers who had broken all the traditions of their culture…. These young women would come up to me and say, "Uncle, don't you understand the meaning of our ideology? Our Cause? The Cause of Liberation for which we will sacrifice our lives."

Ideology? For us, Mohan thought; for my family and myself the only ideology was one of survival. He continued thinking of the regions to which they were being led … had its troubles – destroyed by the political conditions of the times, internecine wars, natural causes, tanks breached by the storm of 1802, … there too, the guerrillas of Pandara the Wanniyar chief pursued their way of life. Survival again – villages at their mercy – lawless times … but for survival. People of the Wanni migrating near the sea coasts and the forts, cultivating and tilling the land ... seeking to some extent, security. Vast forests infested with elephants but the land was still rich. Had potential. It was here that the refugees would move until the crossing at the Kilaly lagoon came to an end. What would be the alternatives? They lived in hope of going back to their old homes, to sort out the wreckage, rebuild their lives. Repair their dismantled, mined homes.

Revathi had loved her home, furnished with the possessions that caught her eye. She had the foresight to send her saris and jewelry to be in the safekeeping of a relation in another village, less close to the war zone. They had left the house with whatever it contained and walked out. The little girl Rhema had got used to bombers that flew over the Peninsula. She would run instinctively along the boundary of the parapet wall of their garden and lie flat on her stomach. Fear was not a feeling she understood. The act of preservation had begun early. Mohan had always ensured that they had stocks of food at home. Plenty of firewood cut and stacked up. The tin of Anchor milk was always full. There was flour too so that they could always make a roti or two. Coconuts they had. From his wife's dowry land in Chavakachcheri. The husband and wife did a little gardening together, peaceful pursuits in the midst of invasions and military occupations.

Fortunately for Mohan, a friend who owned a small tractor had come to his aid. The womenfolk could travel in it while he walked beside it. Walk? A step at a time. The tractor had hardly moved. If it did, it was at the same pace as those who walked. Humanity. Anonymous to the rest of the outside world. The old and the young. The wounded fighters. Not to be left behind. That was all that mattered. Sometimes the entire mass stood still, shoulder to shoulder. The sighing breath, the harsh gasp grazed their sore limbs. Patience. Patience. Then the entire pelt of human beings twitched, shivered as the slow and agonizing movement began. Fear of being crushed to death. If you could no longer go on, left by the wayside. To lay down and die. Still, no one wanted, consciously or voluntarily to die.

So, each step was carefully measured, the entire mass moving with one will.

Mohan felt irritated if anyone jostled him. He heard the murmur of hurtful utterances. Curses. Blaming the Tiger cadres for their plight. In his mind he went over the words of the children of Israel on their exodus. "Would to God we had died by the hand of the Lord in the land of Egypt, where we sat by the flesh pots and when we did eat bread to the full, for ye have brought us forth into this wilderness, to kill this assembly with hunger...." In spite of the fact that they had known so much deprivation through the years of banning certain essential items to the Peninsula, the people could now only utter recrimination against the Tiger cadres. Militants and sometime their families raced along the crowd-packed road regardless of the people. A swathe was cut through the solid, massed wedge in the closely packed ranks. A woman was flung off the road as the phalanx edged each other to the verge. No one went to her rescue. No one bothered to see whether she would rise up and walk. The people moved on. Some stepped off the road, walked in the muddy fields. Wet to the skin. Soaked through as rain fell. There was no pity for a single human soul other than one's own kith or kin. Survival. Against the greatest odds. Bitter recollections of the past. The falling bombs. The perpetual shelling. The shrapnel that tore into the flesh. Sometimes remained embedded within you, became a part of your body. The body now a war zone. The shrapnel could enter in anywhere. No boundaries for those injuries. The body transformed into a military target. Expendable. A man could always carry the war with him. Even until death. A friend had showed Mohan just where the shrapnel had gone in, at the base of the skull. "Let it remain there," the doctor had said, "I won't operate on you. You can live with it. It will become with time, a part of you."

Other images had surfaced in his mind. The young guerrillas walking along the road, trained to take deadly aim at their targets. They were so young yet their life span so short. They carried their machine guns in their hands. As they came upon a mango tree laden with ripe and ripening mangoes Mohan had seen a strange expression cross their faces. It was not the innocence or mischief of childhood. That was perhaps there, buried in some deep recess of their being but it now mingled with the pride in their new skills.

"Look, there's a red one," the young guerrilla had pointed out the fruit. Shot straight at it. Fell to the ground. Whether they had time to eat it or not Mohan never knew. And when they sighted a plane flying overhead the young ones, twelve, thirteen years old, the Baby Brigade they were called, lay instantly on their backs, cradled their machine guns in their arms and splattered the air with a volley of shots. Yes, they had kept on shooting, shooting, shooting into the air.

Mohan had been working in a Christian organization in the town, cycling to work every morning from his home in Mirusuvil. There was nothing that he was not called upon to do anywhere, close at hand. The screams of the dying and the wounded when the bombs fell in the church premises in Navaly missing the military target, still rang in his ears. The scene would remain imprinted in his mind. The civilians had been out in the garden cooking food outdoors for the refugees or just sitting in the shade of trees, talking about what was to happen next. As he went about the dead and dying, his hands and clothes had been covered with blood. The pain of the wounded entered his veins. Their deaths became his, an imagined reenactment of his own which could take place at any moment. Death. He had much time now to think of its everyday aspects. It's commonplace actuality. Mohan had never been afraid to voice his opinions, his thoughts, even among the militant cadres. When the Tigers were taking a man for execution he would say, "Don't drag that man through the market place to his death. Why do you want to kill him before the public eye? At least take him away to a quiet place, out of the public gaze and do what you have to do, if you have justification for doing so." He had often been questioned by interrogators of the Tiger Intelligence, very politely of course. University educated. Knew how to question him with subtlety. Mohan even met the top brass in the Movement. Incidental meeting. The Big Man had come into the Institution where Mohan worked for some reason or another. Offered him a cigarette – that particular brand was something of a luxury for him. Mohan had studied him intently. Not often that these men were either seen or heard. A kind of imprisonment within the Cause? A voluntary exile from everyday life? Inhabiting their lonely islands. Human too. Had a lot of pet dogs. Man with an air of aloofness about him. Exuding a sense of tremendous power. Yes, a very powerful man. Valuable to many of the Superpowers too. Mohan and he had smoked their cigarettes together in silence. One could not go near him usually. And the other, the "Biggest One." His children were brought to school accompanied by their bodyguards. Fear of the enemy within. Power has its vulnerability. Mohan had spoken to one of those bodyguards on the school premises. "Who are you? What are you doing here?" He had asked of him. All the bodyguard had done was to show Mohan the pistol, concealed beneath his shirt, cased in its holster. It was natural that the children of the Leader needed protection. Danger everywhere. Informers. Hostile elements. So, precautions are taken. And the other students? There was weeping and wailing in their homes when they went away with the militants, joined the Movement. Their parents might never see them again. Sometimes they mysteriously appeared again in the classroom. Parents who had influence may have got them out.

Ideology. The Cause. The Movement. Liberation. Martyrdom. Vanati, one of those young women who had fought in the Battle of Pooneryn and died at the age of twenty-seven was also a poet. Left behind poems that spoke volumes of her passion for the Cause. Her bridegroom was Death – Death with whom took place that final and absolute consummation. "She had turned her heart into iron.... How far removed from women like my wife," Mohan had thought. In the Peninsula there was this "Abode of Commemoration" the Ninaivalayam. Dedicated to the LTTE heroes who died at Anaiyirravu especially in the months of June and July 1991. The new women, the young woman, the female fighters. Who had given ear to them? Mohan was used to students, to women like his own wife and mother.... Very different to those poets of the battlefield who wrote their poetry during the interim periods of cease-fires. Those young women had never experienced real peace. Nor any relationship or friendship with the people from the South. Vanati's life was like that last poem which she was never able to complete. Her life story was told by another female fighter, Parati. Both women were killed in battle. All that mattered to them was the liberation of Tamil Eelam. Their deaths were, among their cadres, heroic deaths....

"How could these young people understand my mind?" Mohan often thought to himself. "The mind of a middle-aged man who had traveled all over the world, traversed the face of the globe and returned to the Peninsula, planning to settle down, get a job, marry, have children? My daughter is young, still so young. When she grows up will the war still be on, the burning questions at stake, unresolved? The militants had sacred words. A special language of metaphors with all their connotations. The body of the slain warrior was the seed that will sprout again. And to them, nothing was more sacred than this land which they say is theirs to preserve by the shedding of their blood. They would tell Mohan those things over and over again. Tried to explain their philosophy, the ideology of their Cause. Martyrdom and sacrifice could not be separated from their way of thinking, in the South too, wasn't the life of the soldier who shed his blood for the Motherland seen as a sacrifice? Had the Motherland then become like the goddess Kali? With what ideologies could patriotism, sacrifice, martyrdom be equated? For those in the North, for those in the South war appeared to be approached with a sense of religiosity, the rituals of pooja, of vows and penance."

Mohan felt himself an ordinary man whose life and death would be recorded only in the minds of his own family and his few friends. He was one of those countless, anonymous beings who tried to live his life according to his own personal philosophy and now in this time and place, he had to use all his resources to help his family to come through this ordeal. He had no allegiance to any leader. He had no ideology of his own. All he wanted at this moment was to stay alive and if they all came out of this, begin to take a new route, anywhere, out of all this chaos and turmoil.

Mohan's face was just one in a crowd. As for the leader of the Cause, did he stand out head and shoulders above them all? Was he recognizable? Perhaps Mohan had seen him. Who knows? When he met the priest in the kovil what did he say? "Did you notice that man who just went by?" Passing Mohan by. Passing others by. Not distinguished in any special way. Not in military fatigues ... not traveling in a vehicle ... like a wayfarer, a nondescript wayfarer, a mendicant even. Sadhus and swamis many go unregarded, accepted as part of the landscape ... but for Mohan? There had been priorities. The students. Those who still wanted to study, pass their examinations, enter the Universities in the South or even become ... asylum seekers.... It was his duty to switch on the generator every night in the institution where he worked. The students would gather there to study. There again, until orders were issued that it should come to a stop. Mohan continued his work. Careless of any threat his individual efforts would cause him. He had known, in the course of his life loss, danger. Escaped by the skin of his teeth. Like when he returned by boat from India.

Mohan had spent many years in Europe before finally returning to the island. Had taken the overland route through Eastern Europe, reached Italy through Bulgaria. Traveled with two friends, one a Dutch Burgher, the other, Sinhala. It had been different in those days. Hadn't considered himself an asylum seeker? What had impelled him on that journey? He had fallen out with the principal of the college where he had been the Cricket coach, giving up his job and had decided to try his fortunes abroad.

Led a wanderer's existence for many years. During the latter half of the seventies Mohan had found work on a building site in Turin. Mixing cement. He had found himself very much at home in Turin. There was dignity of labor and the Italians were friendly. He would hang out in the evenings, looking out on the streets, observing the life there. Became friendly with a restaurateur. Washed dishes in his restaurant, learned to cook Italian food. His specialty was pizzas. The owner of the restaurant was impressed with his work, sent him to a Hotel School where he followed a course in hoteliering. He ended up working in the Front Office of a very posh hotel – one which belonged to a chain of hotels in Italy. He was gradually making a life for himself there. He was comfortable. He had his own room with all the amenities, good food, plenty of choice Italian wines, traveled in every part of the country, became fluent in the language.

Mohan felt no need for a special philosophy of life there. Had everything he desired. Spent a year in Malta too. Things were cheap and plentiful in Malta – earned plenty of money, saved some of it and then traveled nearer home, but first back to India where he spent a period of time. And then he was overcome by the urge to come back to the Island – to his home, settle down. But his passport was not in order. Decided not to fly back but to take a boat home, setting out from the southern coast of India. It was on this return journey that the boat was caught in a storm at sea, began to list and keeled over. Mohan and his companions managed to jump onto some rocks. While he perched on that precarious and jagged ledge, waiting, hoping for rescue he felt strongly, perhaps for the first time that this would prove to be a turning point in his life. On one side of the rocky ledge the waves churned and foamed, the ocean here was very deep. The boat acted as a kind of buffer, keeping them away from being inundated and drowned, pulled by its strong currents. Every thing he had, all the money he had saved with which he hoped to start out on life once more, all his clothes, everything, went down beneath the waves. Couldn't salvage a thing. The men had stood on the rocks all night, wet to the skin, chilled to the bone, until the next morning they were able to attract the attention of some fishermen at sea. They were rescued. Life. That was all that mattered.

Mohan returned to his mother's house in the Peninsula, found a job, got married, had a child and lived his own life through invasions and military occupations.

He had now to find the true reasons for his survival. He often thought of those who died from the bombing and the shelling. He was not one of them. He was a survivor. He had now to find the true reasons for his survival. He had not perished when the shells fell on the houses. Not even in the crossfire. "I am destined to live. But why?"– he often thought when he got news of the death of a friend. Perhaps his search for an answer lay here, at this point of time as with his family, they walked out together to join the teeming mass of refugees. The decision was made for him. He would not remain but leave the Peninsula, eventually, create a new kind of freedom for himself and remain anonymously alive. He had spoken to the prisoners who had been released from the jail just opposite his institution, changing their prison garb before they too had set out. "We have been asked to go," they had told him. They too would be part of the exodus.

Mohan's long walk through the evening, through the hours of darkness into dawn, daylight and midday had shown him those stills taken from his life, from his past. His one desire had been to quench his little daughter's thirst when they had arrived at Chavakachcheri.

"My daughter, you will now have as much water as you want," he said, carrying her with great tenderness in his arms.

"Water," she whispered, "water," but she was already asleep as they walked into the midst of the groups of refugees encamped in the garden overflowing from within the house.

The mother-in-law had come running out to greet her daughter and granddaughter. She led them inside her bedroom. There were women and children stretched out on cement floor, sleeping on the beds, crouched in every corner of the room. A small space was cleared for Rhema, a pillow placed beneath her head. She woke up and said "Water, water – thirsty." Her grandmother had brought her a small silver lotah of water and held in to her lips. Then she had laid the child back to sleep, fanning her with the edge of her sari, smoothening out the tangles in her hair.

Mohan walked out into the garden. Refugees. Despair in their expressions and stance.

"From here, where do we go? Where do we go? We have lost everything, No shelter. No homes." The garden resembled a gypsy encampment. Woodsmoke curled up from cooking fires. A mother fed her baby beneath a shady tamarind tree. Men and women, sat around staring into nothingness. Clothes bedraggled. Hair awry. "Life's over for us. No future. Too old. Never thought we would come to this." Heartsick. Woebegone expressions. While they rested, the refugees still streamed along the road past the house, walking, walking, walking.

Mohan had a feeling that their arrival caused a sense of trepidation in the hearts of others who had settled in, transients as they were. Fear of having to sacrifice the precious bit of space they clung to, to sit, or lie, or spread a mat or cloth to lie on. He could read their thoughts ... the daughter of the house has arrived. She and her family are entitled to the best room in the house. We are but outsiders. Temporary guests. We must move out but until we do ... where can we rest? It's too early to set out on the next lap of our journey, face the new uncertainties ... make the crossing ... dangerous ... walk into the desert ... travel into the wilderness. Will our generations ever see the Promised Land? If we are never able to return home where will our funeral pyres be lit? So many deaths ... numberless ... more to come ... of our sons and daughters, while we make the crossing. The Cause will take our sons away from the refugee camps where they will have nothing to do but purposelessly while away the time. Hours filled with frustration. Yes, with the disruption of the schooling they will have no other alternative but to join the Movement. How can we manage for food, for shelter? How long will the little money we have last? We will be forced to sell whatever gold jewelry we have managed to bring with us...."

Ah! Yes, those were the thoughts, some of them unspoken that Mohan shared with the others encamped here. Revathi, his wife had fallen into an exhausted sleep. He walked to the well, changed into an old veshti that his mother-in-law had given him and began to draw the water, pouring bucket after bucket of water on his body. He washed his stained and sweat impregnated clothes and hung them out to dry.

His mother-in-law called him in to drink a cup of hot coriander-flavored coffee. She was silent. Neither of them felt the need to speak. She had already heard everything from the others, thankful for the safe arrival of her daughter and grandchild.

Mohan sat musing on the step, looking out into the crowded garden. He felt he should not cause more unease to these people. They had suffered enough already through their displacement. They must go and stay with his wife's sister for a short time, recover from the effects of the trek and then make the crossing, reach the Wanni area. And from there? To the South for himself, his wife, his child.

Make a new life there. A different life. He had watched the boat caught in the storm, all his possessions carried into the deeps. Kept vigil on the rocky ledge. The night had been dark. The waves had risen high soaking his clothes. He had shivered throughout those long hours. Kept his eyes open. Dared not sit down. Dared not fall asleep. Morning had brought rescue. No, he did not want to return to Europe. He had wanted to come home. There was nowhere else to go except in the direction of the wilderness, feed on its locusts and manna. Which route would lead them all out into the Promised Land? The land flowing with milk and honey. What would they find there? The milk sour? The honey bitter?

THE BRIDGE

The funeral took place with full military honors. I felt myself disembodied, detached from all the rituals of death. I wanted to imagine that it was not my son, Shantha. That it was somebody else's son to whom I need not give even a name. I imagined myself consoling the bereaved, the parents, the kith and kin. It was an act of betrayal. Even of cowardice. The feeling was only momentary. Looking down at that calm and unlined face I stared into the mirror of my own self-image. To deaden the pain, I imagined myself lying in that satin covered coffin surrounded by mourners. Would people regret my passing away, or considering my duty done, as a father, as a useful member of society and a law abiding citizen would they be resigned to the inevitability of my death. The wildest imaginings passed through my mind. No, it was not my son lying there. I wanted bitterly to disown him. I wanted to think that he was still alive. That we reassuringly would hear his voice reaching us through the crackling of wires, that his messages however faint and indistinct would reach us from the operational area he was serving in. We clung to his every word, with all its pauses and interruptions. The sounds of battle, intermittent firing, the thunderous burst of shells heard in the background. Where was this country. Did it have a name? My son a new inhabitant in that wasteland?

Surrounded by my family and friends I had to put on a brave face, to remain calm. The face must not betray my emotion. I would not let that mask crack to show the grimace of pain on my contorted features.

I wanted my senses to be numb. It is easier to be one of the crowd of mourners, to offer sympathy, rather than to receive it, to accept the time-worn phrases of condolence. If only the human touch would wake him. If only I could hear his voice again.... I wanted to cry out, "Puthé, wake up. How long will you be with us this time?" "Father, I have to think of my men. I have a responsibility towards them. They are in my mind from morning to night. They look up to me as their leader, to give them strength – they are human, sometimes lonely, perhaps frightened especially the very young and untrained, inexperienced in battle although they never speak of their fears. I must get back to them as soon as possible. I must return to my regiment early tomorrow. I'll come back as soon as I can." We began to live from one leave to another, those brief and transitory periods during which we wanted to stretch time beyond the limits of hours, days, nights.

Yes, he was a born leader. And duty conscious. Always was. Resembled the other members of my family too, the son in the air force, my daughter, a teacher. They were so concerned, so responsible about their missions, their charges, completing their schedules of work always on time. Had I not been their model from the time they were born till the time they grew up?

No one could read my silent thoughts. Was he finally at peace? No more waking up to the sound of mortar fire and shelling. Of being caught up in land mine explosion or grenade attack. His medals, so many of them, awarded for singular acts of bravery on the battlefield together with the insignia of rank, lie lightly on his breast. His uniform is impeccable, immaculate. Not crumpled and limp with blood and sweat. Uncreased khaki uniform. I contrast my own failure. My own false values. How do I measure courage? Equate it with patriotism? Compel my sons to do what I am no longer capable of? I brought him into this world and signed his death warrant. I had to make a decision at this point. I could not have refused. It was what he wanted. I too perhaps wanted a son who would distinguish himself in the defence of the motherland. As I looked upon that once smiling face, that once firm, wiry body for the last time, I felt a sense of immense loss. The others could continue living. My life was already nearing its end. I did not want to be a wretched, abject human being waking up in the chilling silence of dawn haunted by the specter of my son on whose head I could no longer place the blessings of the Triple Gem. For the rest of my life almsgivings would be planned for his journey through samsara. I had already given the most precious alms I possessed. I decided that my samsaric journey would merge with his.

From what country was his body brought home? Crossing that bridge that linked the passage of our lives, our journeys and destinations. I would often imagine that landscape from what he described. From what he saw and experienced. From the brief flashes on a flickering screen, that we glimpsed. That was the only reality for me. I felt I was watching a war being fought far away in some unknown terrain. This landscape in the village on the banks of the river Mahaweli with its emerald green paddy fields, flowing streams and rivers, blue-green hills and mountain ranges, viharas and temples appeared so untouched, so tranquil. War had ravaged that landscape in the North. You felt the emptiness of death and desolation in those deserted villages. The shells of ruined houses, bullet-pitted walls. The huge palmyrah palms slung like casualties beneath the onslaught of armored tanks that toppled them over, the crumpled fences of dried palmyrah fronds, the camouflaged men.... Strange one never saw the faces of the enemy, only their bodies sprawled in death, limbs outflung, weapons gathered together and placed in neat array. How lonely the men must be from their villages and homes in the South. Trapped within that Peninsula. Not knowing when death would descend on you. My son was an officer. I was so proud of him. Yes, I would often boast of my son who served the motherland but I did not anticipate the sacrifice I would have to make. I cannot bear it. Everyone comments that I am taking it up well but within me, my heart is a leaden weight. I cannot live with my own guilt. I must begin to make my plans ... in secret. To prepare for my own death, the purpose of life over for me.

Shantha, my youngest son, I can never face the rest of this

life, without his presence. Thoughts torment me. I sent him to his death. Of course he went willingly. I wanted him to show us all, his entire family, the glory of war. I wanted to be part of that reflected glory. Now it is all over. With this very hand I signed those papers which gave him the sanctions to choose between life and death. I am now my own judge. I will be my own executioner. Yet even in the way I have chosen to die there is an element of selfishness. Water was always my natural element. It is selfish that I wish to die in this river that flows past our house, feeling the last vestiges of that challenge of the past. My children had clung to my neck as I swam out in the full strength of my youth, into the deepest parts of the water whether it was the river or the ocean. Shantha would cling to my neck. He was so confident in my prowess as a swimmer. He knew that it was my responsibility to bring him back to the safe shore so he held on, his grip tight however deep I ventured out. He was so confident in me. It was I who let him down. I wanted him to feel that war was something glorious. Courage in the field, bravery, heroic acts, fighting to defend the motherland…. Others were making the supreme sacrifice almost daily yet did I imagine that my son would have a charmed life, that all the vows made for his protection, the pirith thread bound round his wrist would save him? We were part of this new band of nameless and anonymous parents, who had to look upon the empty bed, the empty chair, the vacant spaces in our own lives. And to face the bitter truth that all who expressed so much grief and sympathy had to eventually turn away and go back to their own lives. Even my own family. Even Shantha's wife. Whom would his son call "Father," again. In my mind I am haunted by the figures of men in uniform weighed down by their body armor falling dead in that dreadful heat, of exhaustion in that dreadful battle at Elephant Pass ending in a debacle for the Forces from the South. There is no end to the pity and waste of this war. Of any war. Anywhere for that matter. Cut off from the wells of fresh water. Death was so sudden. Yet there were those who would return and who would listen to their tales?

Shantha grew up to be like me. As fathers do, we all want to see our self-image in our sons, that heroic image we imagine ourselves to possess with those inherent qualities of courage, bravery, leadership. We want our sons to wear the medals which signal them out as heroes and leaders of men. I could never wear those medals. I was born at the wrong time. There were no wars in my youth, no battlefield where I could show my prowess by bearing arms for the defence of that noble cause, patriotism, love for my motherland. History has given us a tradition of heroes, not of cowards and this was the strength that I saw in my son. Command. He was the officer in charge of his regiment of men who looked upto him, obeyed him implicitly in their fight against the enemy. In our days we had a different concept of the word "enemy." Moreover he himself had respect for the oneness of purpose that the militants possessed. There was a total commitment to the Cause he would often tell me. And the women too. There was no distinction between men and women when they bore arms. It was difficult for my generation to understand all that my son Shantha said. His fearlessness, his disregard for his own safety counted most together with the ability to command his men, to be responsible for their safety, to uphold them in those moments when their defences would be down. He would never desert his men even for a moment. Did I see him as some Titan battling against lesser beings?

Yes, Shantha had a regiment under his command. He made decisions of life and death. He was not only looked upto by his men but also by the officers of the High Command. He was reputed to be fair and just at all times, never to kill for the sake of killing. Sometimes he could not bear to fire that final shot. To deliver that *coup de grâce*. Did he lack a kind of moral courage? Did he see himself in that man who lay mortally wounded before him, looking at him with death in his eyes? "Finish him off," he would tell one of his men and walk away. Those were his words of command but at that moment did he not shift the burden onto someone else's shoulders? Ironically when he received that fatal sniper bullet no one knew, no one could name that person. He went back into the shadows, was seen and heard no more. They tell me that Shantha's presence among his men was morale raising. There were no deserters from his ranks. On the day of his death which was unpredicted and unforeseen he bad been issued orders to move to another operational area where fierce fighting had suddenly erupted. He had to obey orders. That's where he went to his death. They tell me death was instant. He hadn't a chance of escape. He died a hero's death, they tell me. My other son, Saman, who is a Squadron Leader piloting those Antonovs, Sia Marchettas and Kfir jets, in their conversations together would always say, "The soldier who dies on the battlefield will be remembered to have died a hero's death." "No," Shantha argued back. "No, he will be remembered forever as a fallen hero."

I looked at my son-in-law, Asoka. He is a man of peace. He will never fight for the same Cause that my sons were ready to sacrifice their lives for. He will survive all the mundane vicissitudes of life. He will live to see his children grown-up. He's the kind of man all of us will rely on. The comfort-giver. He will sit by me, persuade me to swallow my pills, to eat, to drink, to keep me going. He will talk to me, listen to me. Nothing will shock him. I cannot expect the others to suspend their lives and be by my side but there are things I cannot tell him, thoughts that begin to rise in my mind. They take me to hospital hoping that I will recover from the physical ailments I suffer from. I cannot eat. Food chokes me when I think of Shantha. He did not have time to have his breakfast before he left for that battlefront. How can I eat when I think of him?

I can't blame the stars for cutting short his life. He and his young wife were always conscious of the uncertainty, the unpredictability of events. Once she made an inexpressible statement. She referred to "my first husband" after they had visited an astrologer. The first husband would be Shantha. It could only mean one thing. I feel a great sense of anger surge within me when I recalled those words. So matter of fact that utterance, so down to earth. But then she was young, she would have to look out for herself; not spend the rest of her life in mourning. She had already lost a brother in the war. She knows the realities of war. There was no place in their lives for the woman who had been the wife, the bereaved one. They would not want any reminders of grief and mourning. My daughter-in-law from the very outset knew that life must go on. She had a young son. She would want other children. I can't have harsh feelings towards her. She and my son married with that monstrous fear looming up before them on a grey horizon. They were already preparing for the inevitable. It's what war does to people. To those who are left behind. They have to grapple with their newly discovered strengths or weaknesses. Strength for the conduct and control of their daily affairs. People will shake you off after the first emotional words of consolation. You will wipe your tears in a silent room, alone, and press your hand against your mouth to stifle the cries and moans of loneliness and grief "You are not the only one who is suffering," I read their silent thoughts. But my wound is one that will never heal. I put on a brave face. People whisper among themselves, "He has taken it up very well."

There's that huge yawning chasm of self. I'm that minute object struggling to reach out of the pit where I've missed my step, fallen in.... I am waiting for that lifeline to pull me up. One part of me wants to reach the open space above, breathe fresh air, look around at the greenness of leaf and foliage but ... then your eyes alight on the grieving mourners, tear-wet cheeks and the weight of guilt pressed you down, down, earthwards. The hard pendulum strikes against your ribs. How can you live with measured time again.... I finally begin to visualize that distant terrain in the North. It's always that part of the map with the thickest, blackest arrows indicating the route of attack, converging on the battle zones ... names tumble through my mind, they are not all blank spaces. Where are the people? Where are they? A haze crosses my eyes. I can only see the gigantic war machines, the spurts of fire reaching beyond a land destroyed and devastated, trampled-down vegetation, the men running, falling flat on their stomachs, firing, then getting up again and running.... The din, the thunder of that artillery fire deafening the ears. The names of the battle zones change but each one of them has gone down in history. My son's body fallen, other nameless bodies fallen. The map of the embattled region grows larger and larger. It covers the whole wall. Spreads and spreads. The news reporters watch impersonally at the routes of attack as the military targets are pointed at by the Commander-in-Chief. I hear that voice, I do not know whom it belongs to, go on and on. The facts so cut and dried. It's like a video game on the screen being manipulated by unseen hands. Planes fly over the Peninsula, bombs fall on their targets, there are numerous conflagrations. No one sees the void, the desolation, the ruins, the broken crushed palmyrah fences. I hold the palms of my hands together and bow my head acknowledging the presence of the living but I am already a dead soul, yes, a dead soul....

He paused only for an instant and then he leaped off the bridge into the water that flowed in such swift currents beneath it. He felt the chill sharp shock of the water slice like knife blades against his weakened body. The water parted like a fissure to receive him and in a swift revelatory flash he thought of his childhood on the banks of the Huluganga, the days of diving and swimming hour after hour, lying on the rocks, basking in the sun, feeling its heat seeping into the skin against the chilled flesh. He had never thought then of death. The river was the source of life. He could try out his strength against its currents. He could feel his body flowing with the river as the blood coursed through his veins.

He allowed the first delight of plunging into the water, of that brief flash of joy overtake him. He began to float, then he gathered whatever strength he had in his limbs and began very slowly, to swim. If he looked back, the bridge still stood there, a bulwark against time. Soon he would lose sight of the bridge. On either side of the river were the steep, tree covered banks. There was still time to swim towards the bank while his strength held out. He was going to give up everything. He was cutting short his life's journey. He did not want to continue living this life in death.

"I am beginning to swallow water, my limbs feel leaden, I don't know for how long I can keep up my strength ... there is a last chance. I am beginning to lose consciousness. I catch a glimpse of a boat. A boat which appears with foreigners from the tourist hotel on the banks of the Mahaweli. The oars almost touch me ... I can reach out ... grasp one of them.... But I am now too weak.... The boatmen can see me now but to drag a water sodden, half drowned body into the boat would shock the pleasure trip of the tourists.... He ignores me.... I choke.... I am going under.... The bridge is a fast vanishing sketch in my mind. Once it marked the passage leading from one life to another. I feel the water covering me like a second skin. It grows tauter, tighter over my body. The decrepitude of age and weakness seem to leave me. As the current grows stronger I feel the powerful urge and thrust that threatens to overpower me. I try weakly to resist it, to challenge the river to prove my old prowess as a swimmer, but gradually give in. It is not only the strength of the currents but that throbbing compulsion of a greater force, death. Shantha no longer clings to my neck, his body holding close to my shoulders, my body carrying his. My body, the bridge and he, the traveler. So easy to give in now. I have no will, no volition to surface. So tired, so weary ... it's a coward's way out ... not like my son's death ... but it is the only way out. I myself had placed that noose round my neck, it tightens, stifles my breath. My limbs bound by ropes of water from which there is no escape sinks into the oblivion I crave so much for, that mindless sleep of death.

THE WISDOM MANTRA

I've learned to laugh at myself finally. Perhaps the laughter was always there but I was too preoccupied with the feeling of angst. And there were plenty of reasons for that. Why, I began to think, after undergoing a series of disastrous happenings, why should I always have to be so serious-minded, so concerned about the state of the world. The state of my inner world too. It took me years to strip off those layers of concealment. Like the dance of the Seven Veils I stood revealed before the mirror of my own confrontation.

I now discover that I find myself much more at ease in a topsy-turvy world not only of my own creation but that of others too. A lesson I gave ear to when my friend Bonell told me that he could never sleep on the mattress placed on his bed in his student apartment in Glasgow. Sometimes I think I would have liked to spend the night peacefully asleep under that bed but that bed had drawers attached to it, a space saver for books, files, clothes. Bonell would place the mattress on the floor, in the middle of the room and from there he could contemplate the universe of the spider spinning its web on the ceiling. An imaginary spider. I never saw one in our apartments in the University Village, only cats and pigeons. In wintertime the cats were always stalking their invisible prey. A faltering bird perhaps. Some of my friends found it impossible to sleep on beds in their rooms. They wanted to set up camp somewhere other than on that bed. To feel they had a stake to their own territory, rather than submit to the order imposed on them by those who felt your head and your feet had to tally in position to all the heads and feet of all the students layered together in that sandwiched cake or sardine-can. The sardine-can of academic fetuses of whom I was one.

Wherever I went I found that there were lessons to be learned. To ensure a stable, sane mind, order was necessary. It was a shock of recognition to learn how important order was in Macbeth's world. I valued my sleep and an easy conscience, so early in life I decided I would never be a flawed hero like Macbeth or a woman who willed her milk to turn to gall like Lady Macbeth's. I was fascinated by the Elizabethan concept of the world of order, the macrocosmic world which we humans inhabited. All should go well if nothing violent disturbed the Divine Order of Kingship and the Divine Right of Kings. The consequences of any disruption were death, upheaval, destruction.

As for myself I've encountered nothing but disorder all along the way. Had I activated it by myself? Deliberately? On my journeys which have taken me off the beaten track? My manner of embarking on those travels has often been haphazard. I love traveling yes, but the magic carpet kind of traveling – without effort, visas, passports, queues at Embassies and High Commissions. Letters which clearly state that I have been invited etc. and that I am not a *persona non grata*. Above suspicion. The subversive mind camouflaged by a bland expression. Then the security checks, getting to the airport on tune, baggage examination. The best traveler I ever met was the Romanian woman writer who stepped out of a revolution off the plane into the New World with just the clothes she wore and a handbag. Whisked off to a thrift shop as soon as she arrived. The thrift shop was home to traveling writers – I bought an expensive Trinka coat of pure wool, German, for five dollars in Iowa City.

It was important to me to have people meet me at the other end and conduct me safely to my destination. And if there's no one, I tend to spend almost all of my precious stipend on cabs. I make friends more often than not with the cabbies. I take down the addresses in my diary with names

like that of Solly Cohen. I listen to life-stories. Who else will?
And write poems on them too. As I tell myself it's someone
else's problem reading the map, what I do is review history,
but between the embarking onto the plane and the arrival at
a destination so much happens. Unexpected things. Do they
happen to others too? Everybody looks so confident.
Seasoned travelers most of them. Others let down their hair
with a vengeance, especially the holidaymakers. Dressed for
the tropics. Flowered shirts. Garlanded with flowers on this
return to their own countries. On the plane too I have unusual
encounters like the woman from my own country living in
England. An emotional encounter with a very unhappy
human being who cried a lot about an unhappy marriage,
taking it out on the child too, a young daughter. I don't
usually talk to anyone on a plane but people strike up
conversations. Met a couple carrying their own sandwiches
and wedding cake too for their daughter's wedding in Dubai.
Then there was the retired planter who kept visiting the
island. Memories, memories of a colonial Ceylon still a part
of his life so much so that he kept returning again and again.
All those journeys so carefully planned. I am generally
packing at the last minute. Someone has reached me at the
nth hour and says, "Come, come to England, come to Italy,
come to Germany." Always a summons and I go. That's why
I remain perpetually in orbit. But what is it about me that
sometimes rouses their suspicions? When I was trying to get
across to Canada to visit my daughter not only did they search
my traveling bag for bombs but my visa too was scrutinized.
The airport authorities were really scared that I'd – a) never
return to Iowa to complete the Writers Program b) never
return to my own country c) try to claim refugee status in
Canada so that I would be another starving mouth to feed at
the Food Bank and d) claim Welfare. I was on tenterhooks.
The plane was about to take off. I hadn't seen my daughter in
years. This was to be only a brief visit. I kept on repeating.

"Look, look, I have no bombs in my bag. Nothing that
will destroy the plane." My possessions were strewn on the

counter. An avant-garde exhibition of "Women's Clothing." The bag was emptied. They couldn't believe that I wanted to return. I was, to them, yet another potential asylum seeker. The grass was so much greener on the other side. They were suspicious of all my travel documents too. Forgeries. All forgeries most probably. Reluctantly they allowed me to repack my bag. Dawoo who had driven us to the airport stood silent and tense at the barrier. I waved to him after the all clear and raced along the passage to the plane. Embarked. I'd made it.

Suspicion. Even an innocent journey is suspect. But as a writer I shall use all this material. These are the rites of the new passage. Valuable material. I'm cast in the role of the court jester. I'm the Fool. The interrogator has to encode my speech. Unconsciously my utterance to him, garbled, may conceal the most complex thoughts. The most profound philosophy.

The man at Heathrow questions me:

"Will you be coming back?"

"Yes." I say. "If I am invited."

My words entail the hope of hospitality freely dispensed. Yet another says –

"So you are a writer?"

"Yes," I say. I must remember to carry a few extra copies of my books to be left on the counter of the customs official. Here, at least, there was a spirit of bonhomie. The official was young. I was a welcome diversion among the other anxious faced children visiting parents and the parents visiting their now affluent children.

For me, laughter was a catharsis. Laughter at myself devoid of self-pity. I created my own roles, roles which I could play out on the stage of the world even if my audience were invisible. It amused me to be the protagonist of my own plots, counterplots, comic relief, interludes and that final dénouement. How else could I reach, with all those hazards and risks along the way, the destinations other people planned for me.

I possessed no great mystique as a writer living in virtual oblivion in a hill-encircled valley which was supposed to be an extinct volcanic crater. I was not really special to anyone. I wasn't even special enough to have a flight booked for me on any other class than economy class. No, never traveled business class for all those literary conferences. No preferential treatment of stewards and stewardresses bringing me trays of gourmet food. Champagne. Caviar. Baskets of grapes, peaches, pears, nectarines, kiwi and what not. With unlimited leg space, deeply reclining seats, innumerable cushions, fleecy blankets. Flanked by secretaries and bodyguards too. But the stewards and stewardresses on economy class were charming – so well groomed, so helpful and meticulous about safety measures that I felt really nervous. I knew that chances of survival were rare in case of a plane crash. I kept looking around for the safety exits and imagined myself crashing into the ocean if my life saving jacket did not function. Or being impaled on needle sharp mountain peak or being swallowed by an anaconda.

I think of my hero, Gimpel, Gimpel the fool – Gimpel, the hero of the story by Isaac Bashevis Singer. I'd take all the negative, horrible experiences in my life and survive even as a victim. I had my own strategies.

There was that one particular journey. I had arrived at the airport passing through all the checkpoints. I was however armed with a dossier of important names in the Ministry of Defence in case I was stopped for questioning on the way. The driver of the vehicle I was traveling in had left all his travel documents, his drivers licence and identity card behind at the daughter's home but we got through because I proclaimed I was a writer. That I was going to attend an International Conference. And the security check said, "Yes, I've heard of you I have seen your name in the local news." That was one important hurdle crossed. At the airport, after bidding goodbye to my husband, I had my bag with its innocuous contents examined, everything displayed, neatly packed with same gorgeous silk garments to wear at Readings. I moved on.

Once more my visa/passport scrutinized. "Please step aside for a moment, Madam. Can you come this way?"

I was led to the office of the Immigration Chief. Flanked by silent but watchful officers. Hauled up before the coals. He turned the pages of my passport and regarded one page in particular with a grave expression.

"Your passport is valid for only one year. Didn't you see this?" He pointed at the written word. "You're a lecturer in English, not a housemaid going to the Middle East. Look, didn't you read this?"

I had been assured that my passport was in order until the millennium. I decided to make an appeal. Not to be self-defensive. My attempts at an explanation made the officer irate. So I had to resort to pleading "I have to represent my country at the Conference. My presentation is for the opening night of Interlit at Nürnberg. They need me...."

"You're giving the keynote address?"

"Yes, I am."

He signed without a murmur. I was on the plane. And then to Frankfurt airport on a passenger cum luggage trolley. It jerked. I nearly fell off but I felt secure for the moment. Friends of mine, hale and hearty some of them often claiming to be invalids were wheeled along the maze of passages in wheelchairs and put aboard safely. Not for me. I'd rather ask for directions all along the way or even hobble to the counter on my two feet. Plain sailing leaves no room for discovery.

At one of the several Lufthansa counters the official looked carefully at the visa/passport, next at me. Gave me a quizzical look.

"So, you're one of those Lankiki?"

"Yes, I am, but don't be anxious. I'm not an asylum seeker. I'm going back."

He gave me a look of pure unbelief.

"Lankiki." I have an identity. The new coinage of international travel. Identity declaration. Asylum seeker. Immigrant. Refugee. Exploring all the escape routes. Fancy myself do I? Troublemaker carrying an invisible map with invisible markers. Detention camp then extradition. Next? I had once met an unlegitimized traveler attempting to enter the country stranded in jail in England. He was in a cell with those who had committed crimes against society. If he hadn't been caught he would have found work in a restaurant serving choice oriental cuisine.

I made it once again. There was an exceptionally beautiful girl, hybrid, at the next counter for the flight to Erlangen. I felt relaxed. Followed after passengers who helped themselves freely to coffee from Espresso machines. We sat in silent camaraderie sipping the hot brew from disposable paper cups. Real coffee. No ersatz stuff like that which was drunk in the years of the Second World War. I had not felt lonely at this airport. There was a scholarly looking man filling page after page in a journal or diary. It was warm with plenty of empty seats. Upstairs on the plane I recognized a fellow writer. She was beautiful. A head of dark curls falling softly about her shoulders. Looked like Elizabeth Taylor. On the plane she draws her fur-edged coat close up to her face and sleeps.

Erlangen. I had a lovely young guide. A young maiden from a German opera. I thought of the song of the Nibelungs. I gave myself up willingly to her safekeeping.

I continued my explorations. Erlangen. Schwabach. Bemburg. Nürnberg. The journey continued. At the Grau Wolf Hotel I ate rye bread and German sausage and wrote poetry in the confines of my bedroom. All the action was at the Theatre Café, eating dolmas, drinking wine, talking endlessly and reading, reading poetry, fiction. Listening to writers from Africa, Asia, Latin America. There was not a single Lankikan face in the audience. I was disappointed. Susanne Gumbaum with her enchanting and enigmatic smile took over my life in Erlangen together with Almut my heroine from the German operas. They filled the as yet unwritten pages of my travel journals. Together with Dieter and Jan whom I can never forgot. The writer/professor who reached me in my empty volcanic crater and Jan his wife, the poet.

The time for return arrived. The Look Homeward Angel

Journey. I was awake the whole night although I had asked for a wake-up call. I wanted to be very, very early. Afraid that the plane would take off without me, Norbert, another friend, also a traveler, drove me through the dark, cold, wet streets. Again we had loads of time till the counters woke up and so we drank coffee and talked of his journeys. We began to say our good byes. I waited to present my visa/passport. A woman pushed in front of me. She knew I would present no opposition.

"I was here before you," she said. I did not protest.

The onlookers were embarrassed. I was after all, a guest in this country, their country.

One last farewell. Norbert the kind, kind Norbert who woke up before dawn, left a young wife and wakeful baby to drive me to the airport, returned to his life.

I was now about to return to mine. We disembarked at Schipol. I searched frantically in my purse. I had either dropped my embarkation card or misplaced it. There was a friendly woman who stood at my elbow and comforted me. She was religious minded and preached a lovely little sermon on the Goodness of God. She walked a little of the way with me.

"God is good," she said. "He will never fail you. I have put my trust all these years in God. Pray to him, He will always be by your side. I must now go ... I am from South America but I live here now, after my marriage, in Germany."

I reached another counter. The airhostess was Indonesian. She too scrutinized my visa. "A moment please," she said. Flicked over the pages of the passport. "I am afraid you can't embark on the flight."

"But I'm going home." Then a sudden thought assailed me. I'm beginning to be afire with the spirit of adventure, the thrill of suspense. Intimations of danger.

"You want to detain me? Why?" I asked pleasantly.

"You haven't got a visa for Heathrow."

"But I don't need a visa for Heathrow. I wasn't even aware there would be a stopover there."

"I'll have to phone London," she rejoins.

I was now ready for anything. Felt elated. What they wanted to do was to turn me into an asylum seeker. If that's what they want I would be their guest I thought to myself.

"Want to put me in a prison cell?" I am equally pleasant and polite.

"Don't look so far ahead," said the groundhostess, in a not so comforting manner. "What are your Dutch prisons like?" I continued. Questioning her filled the cold silence.

"We will have to wait and see ...," she said.

Perhaps I can start my research at The Hague. Find out about those faraway seventeenth century Dutch ancestors who began this genealogy of mine.

I continued. "I've also got to send a fax to my husband. He will be at the airport to meet me." I added, "Well, if I'm not to embark, I'm not to embark." I settled down with my hand luggage. A "Prison Diary" – a long epic poem – I began writing it in my mind.

The lines were buzzing. There was an earnest conversation going on.

I looked out of the enormous glass windows at the airport, planes arriving, planes taking off. Cold. Gray. Dull.

"Your travel agent should have seen to all this –" the groundhostess sounded stern.

At last, the Indonesian girl came up to me and said with a pleasant smile and relief written all over her face.

"You have been granted permission to continue the journey."

The departure hour had been put back. Mystery. I shall learn why later. I began to feel at home among the young Sri Lankan stewards and stewardesses.

I joined the world of happy Dutch holidaymakers who were going to enjoy the sunshine, the beaches. The tea estates, the Five Star and Resort Hotels. The package tours, the ancient artefacts, the search for souvenirs while they toured my country.

"Step aside please."

The black uniformed Dutchwoman looked me over. I accepted meekly, submissively, like Gimpel the Fool, all that was meted out to me. An air of defiance, of bravado, would only get me into deeper waters. Go along with the arbiters of my destiny, accept the contumely, the suspicion until the mantra uttered in my conscience got me safely through. I was innocent of what the airport authorities imagined me to be, that I was traveling under false pretences with an assumed identity. I would make no loud proclamation that my intentions were otherwise. They enjoyed that sense of power over my innocuous self. All that mattered to me was to reach that safe haven, home. Gimpel outdid everyone else by reaching Heaven, leaving his tormentors to face their penance. Gimpel would always be my hero.

I became the cynosure of all eyes.

She frisked me from top to toe. "I am not a terrorist."

"That's what they all say." Her face was grave, unsmiling.

The holidaymakers gazed at me. Some of them looked uneasy. Others sympathetic.

It's either my gold bracelet or watch that has given a suspicious bleep, bleep. It has now become my own one-act play.

She searched everywhere but the nooks and crannies of my mind she would never reach. No one could. No bleep, bleep gave me away to reveal whatever anarchic, radical or subversive thoughts I had hidden away.

I was finally cleared. No bombs. No explosive devices attached to my body. I turned round and faced my audience.

"Did you too think me a terrorist?" I asked dramatically.

Some of the young ones came up to me to smile, talk, speak with friendship newly discovered. Perhaps they too were vastly relieved that I was acquitted at the so public, a trial. We disembarked at Heathrow. I discovered later why the visa was needed. A VIP Minister from my country was embarking there. We were both on our way home. He had been on an important mission in London. No wonder I needed the visa to Heathrow. No wonder there was a delay at

Schipol. No wonder security checks were so tight. So many fearful bomb scares, hijacks, on the way back. False passport, illegal emigrants on the way out.

I bought my favorite Body Shop products at Heathrow. Tea-tree products. My bags were already filled with German chocolate and a battle of Box Boitel wine presented at a poetry reading at Schwabach.

Being a writer doesn't mean anything special if you're seen as what I am. The potential troublemaker. I'm no asylum seeker. I'm no terrorist. I'm no illegal emigrant. I do not have a false passport.

But I find myself more at ease now in this topsy-turvy world of having different identities imposed on me. The next time who knows what I plan to have up my sleeve? I am more convinced now that my hero is Gimpel the Fool.

THE DIVIDING LINE

for Devi

Uncle Johann led you away into a life I could never enter on that journey of separation. Your brown shoulder length hair flowing over your shoulders, your head bowed, your hands so pale, so white, brushing the tears from your eyes. I kept watching you till you were out of sight passing through the doors that took you away while I remained behind in the departure lounge of the airport in Toronto waiting to take my flight back home to the Island. When would we see each other again?

I cannot forget those final gestures of parting. Nor can I forgive myself for leaving you alone in another country where I would see you only in those temporary encounters in time and space. We were following different destinies and different destinations. I recalled that phone call that night in Iowa. At the Mayflower which overlooked that dark river flowing through the park.

"Stay back. Don't return. Throw your passport overboard. What have you got to go back to? The same feelings of fear and tension that almost destroyed all of us? Running. Running, running away from our home. Staying in refugee camps. Displaced."

I shut my ears callously to what I know to be true. The perpetual nightmares of being pursued night after night in my dreams. Awakening to the pounding of my heart. The unreality of daybreak in a strange place not my home. Being hunted down by the faceless pursuer.

"I have to go back. Your sister is still there, alone. I have to return. Settle things."

Throw my passport overboard. Become an anonymous refugee. Who would care anyway. Shackled to my own past. I had to take a step forward and I was hesitant. Reluctant. I now feel the weight of guilt. I realize that you were the stronger and I your mother, the weaker. My weakness stemmed out of a desperate need to find security in what was the known, the familiar. The four walls of my home, the structure that would hold, imprison me but give me an unpredictable safety.

"Some people walk backwards," Mali once told me.

"You know the consequences if you return. It will happen again and yet again. The violence, the fear, the terror. We have all been through it together. Did you feel at home in the refugee camps? Did you think of what we as children felt to be dragged out of our homes, to flee, to be in hiding, to come back to face distrust and suspicion. Or sympathy. Pity. Something we did not want. We will always be children of a divided heritage. We don't belong anywhere." I had put down the phone. I blamed myself for my impulsive marriage into this ethnic community and the violence in which I was now embroiled. My children the victims.

"I'll talk to you later. I'll write to you. We will make suitable arrangements. Give me a little more time. In a few days time I'll fly across to Toronto. We'll meet and talk."

Lost years. Lost lives. We begin to draw the dividing line in our minds.

Here, in this room with its meshed windows which keep out strange looking insects that fly across from the park and the river, I find a sense of reprieve. Once more I have left the country in the very midst of revolution with memories still fresh in my mind of the violence that has overtaken our lives with killings, detention camps, mass graves.

I recall the two visits I had during those times, of new fears and tensions when we had barely got over the ethnic violence of 1983. We had now to adapt to a new era of terror.

The monk Rev. Gnana had brought news of one of my

former students, Amal, who had been arrested and sent to a detention camp.

In the past when Rev. Gnana had visited us, I had offered him dana, filling his almsbowl with food which had been specially prepared for him. He had first delivered a sermon on karma, kama and kamma before he partook of the meal.

This time, the words that precluded his sermon were, "Greed, hatred, delusion."

"These are the reasons for all the evil and moral confusion we are confronted with," he said.

We turned next to the subject of politics.

"Have you any explanation for all these uprisings, the arrests, the killings on both sides, the detention camps?" I had asked him. Amal was an exemplary student. What will be his fate?"

"He had it coming to him. No one can stop these things happening whether it be assassination, death by torture, murder. Do you expect the interrogator to speak politely? In a gentle manner? Do you think they can get the truth in that way? The young man you speak of.... Yes, I know him well too. He has been working for one of the social service organizations, an NGO. A special project, social development of the deprived, the underprivileged. He had explained himself. He showed letters, said he was threatened so he had to do as he was ordered by the Subversives. His story did not really hold water. He had even given his vehicle to distribute leaflets inciting people to rise against the Establishment. Incidentally, there were some police deaths too. Well, the investigations went on but finally, it was found that the letters were from his own typewriter."

"Where is he now?" I asked.

"On the Fourth Floor, taken for interrogation."

"And after that ...?"

"He'll be sent to one of the detention centers." It's a world where it's either you or me. Take a soldier, take a policeman – he knows he can be bumped off at any time so what has he got to lose? And think of the men in the camps. The tension there is evidently apparent. That's why they have an officer's mess and a private's mess. They have to drink to keep their morale high."

"And then, the families of the Security Forces? The men are so far from home, from their wives, their children. You know the psyche of our people ... there are many deserters too. Some of then turn violent when they return to find their women friendly with another man. Shoot the entire lot, woman, lover, her kith and kin or desert rather than go up North, to the battlefront.

"Greed, delusion, hatred," Gnana Thera repeated.

"That's why all this is taking place. And there's another reason too. A monk friend of mine who knows these things and has gone deep into meditation says there are evil forces, bad things happening in the spirit world. Invisible forces. We humans can never see them. The Wars of the Dewas."

"Our conversation has changed so much since our first meeting," I remarked. "Then you talked of kamma, kama, karma."

"You have changed too," he told me. "You look more contented."

"Contented." I thought. "More resignation to my fate after the events of '83. We had survived but with difficulty, all the violence and alienation. We were still often made to feel a people apart....

The day before I had met Kirthi, the boy from India. He had visited us with Khema who had been an undergrad at the University with my daughters. He had taken out a pack of Tarot cards from his pocket.

"I'm Indian," he had said by way of introduction. To me, his face was universal. A beautiful face, alive yet peaceful.

"I practice Zen," he continued. "I have a Zen Karate School. You can come to India and meditate for ten days." He held three cards before me. I had chosen them from the pack. He studied them carefully.

"You're a woman with a strong will. Yet, you are still a child inside. You also love solitude. You are still waiting. You will make the discovery one day. Until then you wait, you search." Kirthi had next arranged the cards in two columns. "You have this and this," he said, "but what are you waiting for?"

Did I myself know? A woman married now for many years who had put the past behind her. No, I didn't know which direction to go in after '83 even though I had gone for a space of time abroad, assumed a new identity. My children were grown-up now. Living their own lives. Thinking independently.

"Perhaps I can go back to my painting ...?"

The cards lie before me. I see myself, my life in them. First a woman with an upright sword. A woman waiting for the seed to grow, plough in hand, patient. A woman in a garden of roses. I couldn't read into the future but I would wait for the interpretation of those symbols in whatever time was left to me.

I turned to Gnana Thera again. We talked of karma and of previous births.

"Perhaps you lived with that man or woman in several consecutive births," he explained. "That's why you can explain these attractions you have for certain people. You may have spent five hundred and seventy consecutive births with this one person."

He regarded me quizzically. He felt that I was still a divided person.

"There are two parts in you," he says, "the spiritual and the sensual."

Perhaps he could help me find a sense of peace within myself.

"I shall come and see you in your mountain refuge," I tell him, wanting to explore that world he had created high up in the Knuckles ranges on an old tea estate. The large sprawling colonial estate bungalow was his sanctuary. It was a terrain covered with wild ferns, flowers of yellow and purple on gnarled bushes, tree ferns, wild orchids, cardamom plants growing on the slopes with their huge canna-like leaves.

I felt sometimes the need to be alone, to meditate in those silent windswept spaces on the mountains. I would move out of the rose garden with its carefully nurtured flowers into those solitary spaces in that wilderness, into silence where no words would hammer at my brain.

I look at the pathraya lying on the table beside the monk. Myself that pathraya, I wanted to empty it of all alms. End my life's journey, that journey in search of alms. Leave the empty almsbowl to rest in the garden, to dry in the sun, all those tempting savors of food after the dana to gradually vanish.

Gnana Thera was continuing his discourse. "Karma. Rebirth. Let me tell you a story.

"The Buddha was walking with his monks. He came to a house where two frail and humble old people lived, an old man and an old woman.

"Welcome my son, at last you have come back. We were waiting and waiting for you. The other monks looked away. They thought to themselves how could these two old people be the parents of the Buddha? He who was the son of the king Suddhodhana. The Buddha turned to them and uttered these words:

"They were my parents in a previous birth."

"The monks were silent at this utterance."

As Gnana Thera ends his story, the image of the pathraya floated before my eyes, levitated, rested in space as if on an invisible cloud. I stretched out my hands. I held it again, feeling my human hungers unappeased. My pilgrimage, my pindapathaya, my search for the charity of alms had not yet ceased. I must find my way along whichever path I take, however much endurance it requires, my journeys end was not yet in sight.

Here in Iowa I sat at my desk – writing. Poems. Plays. For an invisible audience. I am completing my play on our experiences in the refugee camps during the period of ethnic violence.

I sit and recall every single incident. The windows were perpetually closed in the schoolrooms where we had taken shelter but I could see the flaming coronets of flamboyant trees through the glass panes. The flame-red flowers glowed against the grey, smoke-filled skies in that burning city.

Here too, at the Mayflower. I am conscious of windows. Glass panes. A fly trapped in the fine net-like mesh.

People here seek danger. Thrills. The delicious thrill of fear. The urge to leave the safety of the known world by swimming at dead of night across the wide, ink-black Iowa river, the swimmer not even being sure about reaching the safety of the other bank. The icy shock makes water and flesh one.

The night before there were brilliant flares from police cars, illuminating the river Iowa. The waters were indistinguishable from the darkness of the night. A woman looking out of her window had alerted the police that a man had jumped into the river and disappeared. His body a streaking white arrow as he jumped off the bridge. Lost in the darkness of the water.

The police cars had shrieked into the night. No one was to be seen. Water jumping. That's what it was called in Iowa City. A very secret, very private act. The river draws them as it does us. I see the ghosts of the Sioux Indians paddling through the green shadows of the branches overhanging the river. Their spirits linger. Kim, my Korean friend tells me that water is a reflection of the pure, ethereal soul. She gives me a tiny folded tissue paper kite as a gift. A kite packed in a tiny cardboard box. To take it back home and release its soul.

I am warned as I walk through the park. Rape and murder can happen at anytime.

"Don't ever walk alone. It's dangerous." Peter Nazareth tells me.

"But I see men and women jogging through the park all the time," I tell him.

"You must be careful," he insists.

A child had been murdered recently and the man suspected of murdering her was her mother's lover. There are interlopers and intruders who enter the campus. People become suspicious of each other. The young girls, bare shoulders in slinky ball gowns wait on the sidewalks with their beaux laughing and chatting as they wait for the limos to take them for the prom dance.

"Tell me, Peter, what is water jumping?" I ask this gentle, scholarly professor, himself in exile with his wife and family from the Idi Amin regime in Kenya. He and his wife Mary are originally from Goa. Peter and Mary had met us at midnight on our arrival. We had taken a limo from the airport and called them from the Mayflower. They had come rushing to welcome us, meet us. They would be our friends for life, always remembered, always loved.

"Water jumping is what takes place under cover of dark," Peter explains. "A man, enters the park, divests himself of all his clothes, leaves them in a pile beneath a tree and then walks onto the bridge that spans the river. Midway he climbs its railings leaps into the river and swims across its breadth. The waters are icy. Once across he picks up his clothes, dries his body, puts on his clothes, walks away. I think of all those unknown men enveloped in the almost invisible skin of water, feeling themselves swallowed, almost submerged by the surge of the current, drawn along, using all the strength of muscle to swim across. A man could make it or not. It's a risk, through the compulsion of his own blood that he must take. Picking up his clothes once more, it is that necessity to assume a familiar identity briefly shed. And then to walk away, free, purged of the burden of past lives. It is a kind of catharsis for the psyche. The secret is his and no one elses. He doesn't talk about the experience to anybody."

Leaving the refugee camps, coming back to the old life, was it like water jumping for me. Going away from the familiar world and then returning to it, my identity changed. Assuming new personae. Disguises. I would never be the same again. I would spend the rest of my life asking questions. Taking on burdens of guilt. The unforgiven. Sending my daughter into exile.

The phone keeps ringing in my mind.

"Throw your passport away. Don't go back." She, my

daughter had made the difficult decision. Only she would know what it would be to confront that gruelling interrogation facing all those who sought asylum in a new land.

"Why do you want to stay in this country?"

"Why don't you want to return?"

Questions asked of a million anonymous strangers.

Memories were bitter in her mind.

Look back into the past.

The mobs had come to our gates that morning – hundreds of them. She and her sister had escaped through the back door throwing away the clothes they wore, clothes that hampered them, into an empty flowerpot and clambered up the steep earth bank behind the house. They had stood at the door of a friend and neighbor, silently pleading for asylum. Asylum. That was the first stopover in that long journey into exile. What she and her sister had feared most was being raped.

We had been taken to other temporary stopovers in the burning township and a day later we found ourselves in our first safe haven of the camps.

It was now someone else's responsibility to protect us. It was there that I felt that aura of power emanating from the man who walked among us with his gun. I had met him briefly before. In my brother's office where he visited us. When we had escaped and taken shelter from the mobs. He was in full uniform. He represented the State. "I am your protector." He told us. "You have nothing to fear." Colonel Ananda. A powerful man. The man with a gun. He was constantly in our midst in the camp. A presence. A power. He exuded it. Power. I could smell its strong odor. A pervasive odor. Compounded of the texture of his skin, the texture of his khaki uniform. Breathing through its pores.

One day Colonel Ananda would go back into the shadows. We would never meet him again but he would not be forgotten as long as we lived. He was more powerful than all the others. The DIG. The volunteer teacher, security personnel. The helpers. The sympathizers. The priests of the various religious organizations.

I felt crazy with all those masquerades. I wanted to remain with my husband and children. I did not want to be separated from them even for a moment. It was inhuman, degrading, to walk into this no man's land where already the victims themselves had set their boundaries even within the confines of this schoolroom.

My past life as a teacher appeared farcical. Tight-lipped, silent police officers had brought us here in a van. When we arrived we found the place crowded with streams of people with desperate faces. The lobby of this huge Girl's School was crowded with masses of people standing shoulder to shoulder sharing the same labored breath. The corridors were chockablock. The classrooms were all occupied. So was the school hall. Even the dais was filled with people. People were milling around in the courtyard too. We would have to find a space somewhere for ourselves.

I kept recalling the telephone conversation with the Roman Catholic Bishop in our township. All the advice he could give us. "It is best to inform the police of your plight and ask them to arrange a place for you to be safe in."

Could he have offered us sanctuary. Wasn't the church always considered a place where the pursued would find a refuge? If he had, perhaps the Cathedral and the living quarters of the priests would have been stormed.

Masquerades. We could have worn the disguises of priests, nuns, acolytes. What crazy ideas to have.

I began to listen to the fragmented narratives of escape that eddied around me. And I began to think of our escape. The beginning of our exile away from the rest of humanity.

For me it was like crossing a frontier from one country to another. A form of migration. Our arrival was not by ship or by air or on the magic carpet of Laila and Majnu. We stepped into unfamiliar territory without a passport. Anonymous people with our lost identities, stepping into a country which as yet we cannot name. We are all poverty stricken in spirit. We have only our thoughts, dreams, nightmares. The horror of filth and faeces. The hovering bluebottle that lingers like an emissary reluctant to leave this thriving community. Humiliation and degradation. The rags of our identities can barely cover our nakedness. The ultimate victory is to emerge out of the pit of horror without a sense of self-pity. In that way we will save our souls. The outrage, the anger and hurt become a spent force behind these barriers that divide us. Keep us hemmed in. Cooped in. We rename ourselves from the tattered remains of our identities.

Here in this camp it did not matter who you were or what you were. I looked around me. The latecomers who had become the less privileged lined the corridors, seated or standing back to the wall. Resignation was writ all over their faces. Families camp everywhere. Husbands, wives, children, grandparents, uncles, aunts. What a commonality of spirit. In the classrooms some kind of organization does exist.

Human nature had tried its best to create order out of chaos. Marking out territory. Creating boundaries through their own personal politics. And petty demographic communities.

I was filled with a sense of anger and disgust at the selfishness of a group of nurses from a private nursing home with religious affiliations. They had demarcated their own private space within a barricade of furniture. Their personal belongings spread out on that half wall of chairs, and desks, clothes, towels, sheets. They were slicing bread on a desk and drinking cups of tea. There was no welcome at our entrance, that of my husband, myself, my daughters. They looked away from us. Our presence was an intrusion. Soon they too would be crowded out. The barricades, so fragile, so impermanent, removed. They would have to huddle together in a corner of the classroom.

Below the stairs in the big Assembly Hall that was already crowded, the refugees from the plantation line rooms were brought in, bus after bus.

There was not a drop of milk for the children. There was no food. No drinking water. Human cargo in the fetid holds of ships. Retching with the lurch of the vessel.

What a sigh of relief I had heaved as I lay down the few

knotted bundles of clothes and linen I had brought with me. We spread some sheets on the cement floor still covered in corners with chalk dust. I felt the chill of the cold cement creep into my flesh. Yet a sense of great and tranquil peace flowed over me. I began keeping a diary in my mind. Waiting ... waiting....

One day when the clamor of the day was dying down I saw that man seated in a lotus posture in a secluded corner of the corridor. It took me back to those days when we walked down to the sea in the North of the island on one of our unforgettable holidays. We had walked day after day through that landscape of cacti, wild custard-apple trees, pomegranate, thorn bushes and palmyrah palms.

Those landscapes kept recurring in my dreams in the crowded schoolroom with its shuttered windows and bodies huddled together in every available bit of space on the floor. A weak bulb glowed suspended from the ceiling. I stayed still so as not to disturb the others but my thoughts writhed in an agony of restlessness. I felt I had no future. There was no world I could walk back into. Marked out. A stranger.

We had to talk. Find people to talk to. Listen. Looking at that calm and tranquil face I asked myself whether it was a face I would want to paint. Have that portrait on my wall. When I was young I had painted many portraits but those portraits were lost, the faces forgotten.

I was drinking from a bowl of fresh, clear water. Water was precious in this camp. While I drank my face looked back at me. Haggard. Unkempt hair straggling on my brow. It was the only mirror I looked into. I bent down and offered him the bowl of water. My face was joined by his. Two faces like blurred shadows.

"We have to go back into the world we left," he spoke the words softly under his breath. "Yes, I know it," I whispered.

Here there are boundaries which we do not transgress. It is easy to live in peace. Because we follow the rules, intimacy does not become familiarity even though we live so close to each other. The stranger will remain the stranger for all time.

You are not a prisoner here. You can walk out if you wish. You have to set yourself free, within yourself find freedom or you can carry your prison cell with you wherever you go.

"If you find yourself in a dark forest in a lonely place, lost, first ask yourself what there is to fear. The silence, the darkness, hidden predators?" His voice murmured softly.

"In the jungle from which I have come it is the fear of humans. It is the cold sweat in my armpit and the thunderous beat of my heart, the cold steel at my throat or the rock hurled at the walls of my home, the crash of tiles, the smell of burning...," I answered.

"But you will come out of the jungle. You will find a path. Follow it till you reach your destination."

How tempting it is to follow his way of life. His fine-boned hands will always lift a bowl of water to his lips or a mug of plain tea as if it were the elixir of life. He smiles, takes a sip or two of water and hands the bowl back to me. Does he think I am the thirstier of the two? Drinking from this shared bowl of water makes us one in suffering. He shows me that there is a way out, to ultimate release.

For some time to come till we move to the next camp and the next there are unwritten rules to be followed. First you fit your life into a minimal space. You learn not to spread yourself or your belongings. There are invisible frames drawn round you. Dividing lines. Boundaries.

You learn that there is power in the silence of sitting, observing, thinking. It is a meditative process. You watch the movements of bodies. This is not a place you will inhabit for long. You will have to move on. There are no walls to hang your paintings on. No pegs. No hangers for clothes. I lived in the clothes I came in. My hair grew snarled and tangled. There were no screens to conceal the naked body. Only the cover of dark to escape into....

We came out of the camps one day, crossing that invisible line. It had seemed a lifetime. We lived briefly together but the time came for our several departures. The decisions to remain or go away forever. My daughter went away alone first on one journey from which she returned temporarily and then she embarked on another and crossed that bridge to another world far from home.

It was in Iowa that I had to make that decision. While I was in Iowa, I took a plane to Toronto to be with her. At the small local airport I was interrogated. "Will you claim asylum in Toronto? Will you return? Will you too join the thousands of asylum seekers in Canada?" I kept reassuring them that I would come back. That I had a program to complete. They would not believe me. Not only was I a potential asylum seeker but I was also a potential terrorist. My bags were x-rayed for bombs. Kept back, almost missing the flight. Raked over by suspicious eyes and finally set free to go my way.

My daughter was now a student at the University of Toronto and working part time in the University Library. We had looked forward to this reunion so much, after years of separation. We had to wait until evening to meet her when she returned from work. We were met at the airport by Uncle Johann, the Dutch husband of one of the cousins, accompanied by Bernice – her smile had a special kind of warmth though it was the first time that we were meeting.

We were to discover long lost cousins into whose lives my daughter has now entered, who entertained us with lavish hospitality in their home, the home they were so proud of. They were the new emigrants. Everywhere we went we were conscious of them. The political refugees, asylum seekers, or those searching for a better way of life with illusions of more comforts than they had back home, jobs, money, education, ownership of houses and property, material possessions. Many of them ended up here as security men, up all night, waiting at icy bus stops in freezing winter, wrapped up in overcoats, mufflers and woollen caps, changing their sleep patterns, anticipating bonuses and OT, signing up for those extra dollars crisp against the palm. My cousin's wife Bernice worked in a big hospital where she operated the giant washing machines, laundering hospital linen to snowy whiteness night after night. She was proud of being given so much responsibility, in charge of giving out linen, sheets, pillow cases, towels, for the patients in the hospital.

The sleepless nights took their toll. They were stressed out. Dark shadows appeared under the tired eyes and yet they felt they had made it, had resident visas, Canadian citizenship rights. Bernice led me to the master bedroom where the brand new bedroom suite filled the space, the double bed covered with its Chinese bedspread embellished with huge quilted roses. "It was a bargain," she told me, "two hundred dollars. I bought it for my daughter. For when she comes with her family, I'll try to sponsor her. I miss my grandson," she added wistfully.

We walked round the house. Everything was spick and span, brand new, in the living room, the suite was five thousand dollars. Vases were filled with brilliant hued artificial flowers, flowers that would never wilt, colors that would never fade. Stems would not soak in staling water. The tabletop was immaculate, shining, veneered. Bunches of iris, narcissi, filled the glass vases. I was reminded of Greek myths and legends.

Bernice talked of extensions to house and garden, of the basement apartment which lay vacant, being kept for her daughter. Those apartments are very common here and can be let out for six hundred dollars or more. I was careful to remove my shoes, as I trod barefoot on the plush carpets. And I listened.

"Nothing like home. I miss the old place," Cedric said as he sipped his whiskey. Exiled now in the autumn of his life he recollected the past, the days before migration. "It was an easy life. Wasn't tied down to anything. Watching TV, talking to the villagers. I had time on my hands. We had this huge estate at Kekenadura, could live off it...." His maternal grandfather Buultjens had owned vast tracts of lands in the South. He had been a scholar of Buddhism and had translated Pali texts and the great Pali canon, the *Visuddhi Maga*. Yes, Cedric and that family had been accepted, recognized, looked upto. You had only to mention the name and everyone in that village in the South knew the family history but here, no one clung to personal family histories. The emigrant was the escapee of violent epochs. He became the common man, everyman in this new country. There was no heroic image left to cling to. No Pali canon to translate. He created his own literature, the minuscule epics of the ordinary man, the day to day saga of the anonymous citizen. Yet when he turned his face towards me I recognized myself in him. I experienced his angst. There was some ancient bloodline somewhere. I was still to discover where, at what point of time it all began, with that unknown voyage, the historical colonial adventure which made us recognizable. My long lost, distant cousin's patois, had not changed. Nor his thoughts. His chilled flesh longed for that lost warmth in that island he had left behind.

We sat down to eat. Bernice had cooked the meal for us. My daughter was at work. The table was spread with a feast of food, chicken curry, yellow rice, potato badun, aubergine fried and cooked, bowls of salad, bottles of wine. Hesperidean apples, candelabras of grapes, green, black; cognac, Bordeaux. We talked endlessly and ate as we did at home, with our fingers.

We went back to Willowdale where my daughter stayed with Cedric's sister Gladys, yet another cousin. We counted the hours for our daughter's return, her step on the threshold, the ring of the doorbell, her excited voice calling out to us as we sprang to our feet, to welcome each other, the warm embraces we exchanged after our separation.

That evening she took us in the buses and through the subways to Gerard Street. As the bus crowded with Chinese women we heard Hokkien and Mandarin dialects which my daughter was now able to recognize. They carried woven cane baskets overflowing with spring onions, jade green Chinese cabbage shading into white, Bok Choy, oblong parcels of crab, fish, noodle packets. I felt like an ant crawling on the Great Wall which stretched in my mind in this city of Toronto, searching for grains of sugar and salt. A survivor like all these people who accepted me, made me feel I was not an outsider.

The streets we passed through were flooded with flashing neon lights and when we stepped into Gerard Street we felt we were in a street in Mumbai with Hindi music resounding from every corner, the wide open silk shops, the Indian restaurants and cafés. We walked among the teeming crowds mingling with men in well cut suits, western attire, and women in sparkling saris of satin and silk and georgette embellished with embroidery in silk, sequins and jari. This was a little India, where the feeling of home and country could be created to dispel the sadness and loneliness of being in exile. Spice bags of voices spilled out of every shop. Aromas of food wafted from the restaurants. The songs were familiar, the voice of Lata Mangeshkar, lyrical, haunting following us wherever we went.

A man sidled upto us in a shop and said, recognizing from where we were, "I know your country. I was there." Connections and links are forged, fragile, tenuous but they hold in these brief encounters.

Another comes up and says, "My father was a milkman in Sri Lanka. I know the Pettah area. Kayman's Gate. Business History. Old landmarks to establish identity." Loneliness is dispelled with a voice that mentions significant places on a map that still exists in the mind. Kinship and bonding are established even in exile. Kayman's Gate. The Pettah. Gerard Street, Harbor Front. The map unfolded. We stretched it out on the walls of our minds. We will return. He will stay on. Yet we would never forget each other. Our daughter was the guide. We trusted her knowledge of the new routes. We feel safe with her. She would steer us with confidence through unknown streets. She was now no stranger to this new world. And yet once I had held out my hand to help her cross the roads we traversed in the country of her birth.

In the silk shop I bought saris to take back home as gifts. I watch a middle aged woman with her family, shopping, piles of Indian silks spilling over the counter. The unknown women, perhaps a visitor like myself, wore heavy shoes and socks, a thick winter overcoat, the hem of a silk sari peeped beneath the coat. Identity was only superficially concealed. Disguise or protection or both.

A drift of silk touched my shoulders. Fragrance of jasmine and sandalwood drifted into my nostrils from the burning joss sticks. And attar of roses. I think of the old colonial novels, the romantic nineteenth century novels ... rose attar, sprinkled at celebrations, Maharajah palaces, zenanas, tiger trophies, polo games ... I am brought back to reality as voices, familiar, caressed my cheeks with warmth. Memory was no stranger that tapped my shoulder but only a long lost friend that greeted me.

"Are you hungry, ma?" My daughter asked me. "What would you like to eat? Dosai? They make lovely paper dosai at this restaurant." We entered a restaurant. The tables were crowded with diners. Bowls and platters of food were carried from table to table. We ate hot crisp paper dosai like enormous folded cone manuscripts on which I inscribed the delicate etchings of hunger. Outside the kitchen a woman stood casually as she would be in her own kitchen at home, resting one foot comfortably for support against the wall, chatting as she sliced a pile of carrots by hand.

"Let's eat upstairs, ma. The toilets are downstairs." This could be a familiar scene at home. Here the natives are the aliens. Here, one white couple stood out in the crowd. We are no strangers. We felt the bloodstream, the flow of rivers, the flatness of plain and valley breathed within the consciousness, blotted out, enfolded in darkness.

We met old friends. "Don't you remember him ma, don't you remember him, dad? He was lecturing in economics in the University of Peradeniya. So many old friends were now resident in Toronto and all they wanted to tell us were their life stories in voices heavy with longing and nostalgia for home.

I did not want the hours to end. The time to pass. I did not want to pack my bags and go away. Then why did I do it?

"We are giving you your visa. Don't let us down. You must return. We trust you," that's what they had said at the US Embassy.

"You are valuable to us as a writer. We don't want to lose you. We need you," says another. A recorder. A witness. That's how they see me.

Now I know, now I experience the excruciating pangs of loneliness, if only I could pack a bag and walk out of my old life. I now have the freedom to do so but my daughter has a life of her own. I listen and listen to all her stories, the harrowing stories of broken families, one-parent families, children who have many different fathers, drug addict mothers, alcoholic husbands, battered wives. Starving people at Daily Bread where my daughter does voluntary work. She meets hungry people for whom the chef cooks and cooks and cooks in his little kitchen – casseroles, pasta, baked chicken – food, food, food.

We talk of the lonely people in the city, of asylum seekers, immigrants and refugees. Also of her life, her friendships, her joys and pleasures, reading all the new books that appear on the shelves, eating at Indian and Sri Lankan restaurants, workouts at the gym.

"In spite of everything ma," my daughter says, "life is good over here." We are both witnesses and recorders of different lives yet we have finally bridged that gap. We understand each other now. I gave her what she valued most, the right to her own freedom, no longer manacled by the outmoded heritage of a lost inheritance.

Our reunion was full of joy. Full of excitement. We spent so brief a time together, three or four glorious days of happiness. Her father who had accompanied me on the journey cooked the food she must have missed. Chicken curry, roast chicken, rice. We walked through the malls, ate Chinese food and heard the familiar voices of young men from home, Tamil voices, Sinhala voices as they passed by, totally absorbed in their own lives, free to walk among those whom they were divided from in their own country.

I have now to wait at airports for my daughter's arrival. At the same time my mind races ahead, filling in blank dates on the calendar, dreading the parting at her departure.

When she returns we sit for hours drinking coffee and talking endlessly of that other life in another country. For her there are now new impressions to be gathered. New experiences. We spend days in the home of Nimal and Mali in Colombo. We drive everywhere chauffeured by Chandraratne or Thushara. She looks silently out of the window watching the young soldiers at the numerous checkpoints in the city surrounded by piled up sandbags.

We go to the kovil for special poojas. We stand in a miasma of camphor and incense. My daughter writes poem after poem which she leaves behind, which I take up, read, put away together with her stories. Poems which mirror the dangers and fears, the hidden tensions, the alienation she felt as a teenager in the campus. The feeling has never left her. Insecurity, the unstable earth shaking beneath our tread as we flee from our homes. Poems like the ones I keep on my desk, in my files, which I read from time to time so that her impressions burn their words into my skull.

ON MY RETURN

On my return I find
the way to Sivan kovil
precarious.
Pettah. 6 PM. Fresh faced
boys strut, guns cocked
barbed wire defences, abandoned

buildings, lonely alleyways
Settling down for night
rags pulled over for cover
People prepare to sleep.

Bells jingle, freed from slaughter
cows breathe relief I choke on
camphor, a priest performs

abishekam, the crick crack of
coconuts, juices refresh the
tired traveler.

In Pettah, wonder when they'll see the
Front. Bodies spliced from limbs,
flesh moves with earth.
Few return whole.

She was on holiday in that beach resort in the South with
Christine, Sarath and their children. When that huge
cataclysmic bomb went off blasting the Dalada Maligawa,
killing the early morning dana givers who brought milk to the
temple. The bomb that blasted the roof of St. Paul's Cathedral
shattering the centuries old stained glass windows showering
the ancient colonial pews with splinters of rainbow colors.

The mobs were out on the roads again. I felt the rank taste
of fear once more in my mouth. The day turned dark, the
sunlight hidden in grey clouds. I stood at the gate, a fish
agape, watching the men with their rough sticks and long
poles walking down the street screaming vengeance. Tear gas
canisters were flung in the air to disperse the men who ran
wild eyed with tears streaming down their cheeks. Scattering.
Confused. I wanted to offer them water to dispel the burning
sensation they must have felt.

"Life is over, life is over. It has happened again. Sleepless
nights. Torturous dreams. Will my daughter be safe in the
South," thoughts raced through my mind as it went back to
the past, to the mobs, to the burning streets, to the camps. I'll
never return," my daughter told me when we were reunited.
"And you? It was your decision to come back."

I had asked for it. I'll never be safe. Never. But then was
there any corner of the world that would remain safe forever?
The most unassailable structure would not be safe. The fires
would envelop even the seemingly stable cities and those
enormous structures and towers crumble and fall burying
civilization in the appalling ruins.

We looked into each others eyes. My daughter consoled me. "Don't feel guilty, ma," she said absolving me from the guilt that burdened my thoughts and life. "It would have happened anyway. I would have gone away for higher studies. I would not have returned."

And yet, I wait and wait. For letters, for phone calls, for the sound of her voice, for the stories she tells me. We have all become spinners of endless sagas which we read in the silence of our eternal loneliness. Surrounded by partings, longing to see each others faces, hear each others voices, we inhabit the world of the exile which lies within the Babylon of ourselves.

ABOUT THE AUTHOR

Jean Arasanayagam was born into one of Sri Lanka's minority communities, and married into another. By birth she is a "Dutch Burgher" – offspring of intermarriages between Dutchmen and women of the indigenous communities – a split inheritance. She herself married a Tamil, and this marriage proved to be totally unacceptable to her husband's family. In July 1983, the antagonism between Sri Lanka's Tamil minority and its Sinhalese majority culminated in bloody riots. Her family became refugees. Jean Arasanayagam bore a writer's testimony of these events.

Jean is an eminent short story writer. Her volumes of short stories are *The Cry of the Kite* (1984), *Fragments of a Journey* (1992), *All Is Burning* (1995), and *Peacocks and Dreams* (1996), which won her a prize for non-fiction in 1984 but was not published until twelve years later.